P9-DWS-301

ANNAPURNA

50 Years of
Expeditions
in the
Death Zone

■

REINHOLD
MESSNER

Translated by Tim Carruthers

ANNAPURNA

THE MOUNTAINEERS BOOKS

Published by
The Mountaineers Books
1001 SW Klickitat Way, Suite 201
Seattle, WA 98134

© 2000 by Reinhold Messner

First North American edition, 2000

Originally published in German by
BLV Verlagsgesellschaft mbH,
80797, Munich
© 2000

Manufactured in the United States of America

Project Editor: Kathleen Cubley
Editor: Kris Fulsaas
Designer: Pam Hidaka
Layout: Paul Carew

Photo Credits: Chris Bonington: 92, 93; Maurice Herzog: 14, 163; Marcel Ichac: 47; Norbert Joos: 19, 95, 100–101, 102, 104, 105, 170, 174 top; Josef Nežerka: 141, 144; Jiři Novek: 177, 183; Jordi Pons: 22, 173 top. All other photographs are taken from Reinhold Messner's library and archives.

Cover photographs: *Top:* Annapurna in the last light of day; *bottom:* View past the South Face toward Annapurna II, Peak 29 and Manaslu.

Library of Congress Cataloging-in-Publication Data
Messner, Reinhold, 1944-
  [Annapurna. English]
  Annapurna : 50 years of expeditions into the death zone / Reinhold Messner.— 1st North American ed.
    p. cm.
Originally published in German by BLV Verlagsgescellschaft in 2000.
  ISBN 0-89886-738-X
  1. Mountaineering—Nepal—Annapurna—History. I. Title: 50 years of expeditions into the death zone. II. Title.
  GV199.44.N462 A565513 2000
  796.52'2'095496—dc21
                                        00-010598

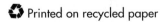

For Maurice Herzog

CONTENTS

MY ROUTE

FROM THE WEST-NORTHWEST

New Routes (Photo Section 2)

FACTS AND DATES

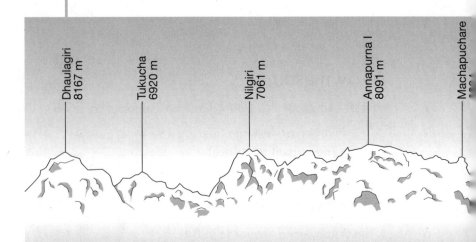

Dhaulagiri 8167 m   Tukucha 6920 m   Nilgiri 7061 m   Annapurna I 8091 m   Machapuchare

"And so, as the dream faded,
we returned to earth in a fearful mix-up
of pain and joy,
heroism and cowardice,
sun and mud,
grandeur and meanness."

— Lionel Terray,
Conquistadors of the Useless

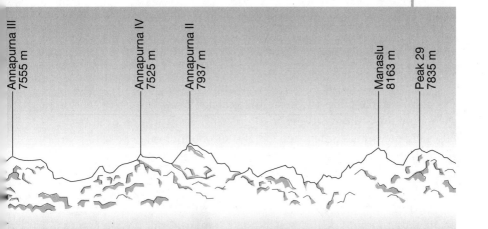

CALCULATED RISK AND THE DEATH ZONE

It is almost as if Annapurna fits uneasily into the modern age, for nowadays, when even dangerous ascents on the highest mountains can be preprepared for those clients with little experience but plenty of purchasing power, this 26,000-foot (8000-m) peak is still regarded as a difficult mountain to climb. You cannot book an ascent of Annapurna through a travel agent—not yet, luckily! From the north the mountain is too dangerous for a guided group tour, from the south it is too difficult, and from the west it is both too dangerous and too difficult at the same time.

When, after a fruitless attempt to climb the neighboring Dhaulagiri, the elite of the French postwar alpinists turned their attentions to the then-unexplored Annapurna, the first thing they had to do was find an approach route to the mountain. Only then could they begin to try to identify a possible route of ascent, develop the logistics necessary for a summit push, and finally summon the courage to climb up into the Death Zone, where there could be no hope of either recuperation or help from below.

So what was known about this mountain in those days, apart from its name? What was understood of altitude sickness and acclimatization? Very little—in fact, almost nothing. No one had thus far reached the summit of an eight-thousander, and much of the experience that had been gained had been lost again during the Second World War.

Although the expedition leader, Maurice Herzog, and his companion, the unforgettable Louis Lachenal, did manage finally to get to the top of the mountain without oxygen masks, their descent was reduced by frostbite, falls, new snow, avalanches, fog, and snow blindness to a crazed stumble through the Death Zone. It was only with great good fortune that the men managed to find their way back to the people in the valleys below, to return to civilization.

There is a difference whether someone reaches the 26,000-foot (8000-m) mark or the actual summit of a 26,000-foot (8000-m) peak, for it is the summit of such mountains that causes the psyche of the person ascending them to change; up there, one is often so absorbed, so forgetful, that the way back down can no longer be found. It is only on the descent that the climber's safety and prudence really show through, and the only ones who truly appreciate just how dangerous these high mountains can be are those who have returned again and again from the Death Zone.

So fifty-six years ago, there was practically nothing at all known about the dangers of and survival in the Death Zone. Each expedition to an eight-thousander was a dangerous experiment, a walk along the knife-edge between life and death. All this is important for a full understanding of Herzog's approach. It was in a spirit of naivety and enthusiasm that this man Herzog led his team to the summit; he was the first to set foot on the top, and on the descent it was he who on several occasions found himself with one foot in the grave. Yet there can be no blame attached to him, and in the end his success was to be enjoyed by mountaineers everywhere, even those who had not taken part in the 1950 Annapurna Expedition. For it was only from the energy created by trial and error, between knowledge and calculated risk-taking, that the treasure-trove of experience could be drawn that in later years was to become accessible to all high-altitude mountaineers, right up to this day.

Now, more than fifty years later in the third millennium, a success such as that of 1950 would no longer be worth even a footnote in the Annapurna chronicle, and a descent made under similar circumstances to Herzog's would occasion nothing more than a bewildered shake of the head; yet Herzog's expedition remains a milestone in high-altitude mountaineering, and a pointer to the future. "Who dares, wins," was how Sir Edmund Hillary described the process of amassing the requisite experience.

It was only in 1970, fully twenty years after the first ascent, that the British managed to make the second ascent of the French Route, and a few days later, a team from that very bold Southwest Face expedition led by Chris Bonington reached the summit for the third time, after Dougal Haston and Don Whillans had climbed the 11,500-foot (3500-m) face. Theirs was the first ascent of one of the big faces on an eight-thousander, and it ushered in the second phase of high-altitude mountaineering, in which the pursuit of difficulty was the name of the game.

In the intervening period, a half dozen independent routes have been established on the South Face alone, together with a host of variations. In 1984, when "minimalist mountaineering" had seen success on the highest summits of the world, Erhard Loretan and Norbert Joos made a complete traverse of the Annapurna I massif, from the southeast to the northwest.

After the ascents of the Northwest Face in 1985 and the Northwest Buttress in 1996, the three Annapurna summits of the main massif were reckoned to be "worked out." Many expeditions failed in their attempts to repeat one of the three big Annapurna faces, and again and again there were deaths on the mountain. Nevertheless, attempts continue to be made, and the mountain sees its fair share of both success and tragedy. Up to the autumn of 1999, 101 men and 5 women had stood on the summit of Annapurna, while 48 men and 3 women had lost their lives on the mountain. The history of climbing on Annapurna is not yet complete; it will go on and continue to excite us, as long as we refrain from equipping this mountain with a permanent infrastructure. This move would both belittle the mountain and dull the attraction it has always held for us—forever.

FROM THE NORTH

The glaciated North Face of Annapurna I, with the East, Middle, and Main Summits visible—the Death Zone

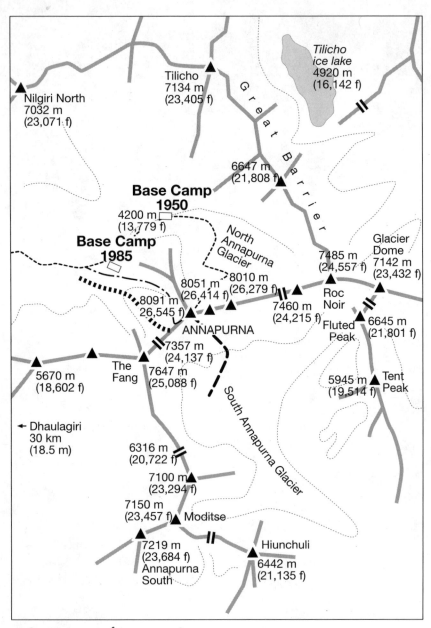

Nilgiri North
7032 m
(23,071 f)

Tilicho
7134 m
(23,405 f)

Tilicho
ice lake
4920 m
(16,142 f)

Great Barrier

6647 m
(21,808 f)

**Base Camp
1950**
4200 m
(13,779 f)

**Base Camp
1985**

North
Annapurna
Glacier

8010 m
(26,279 f)

8051 m
(26,414 f)

7485 m
(24,557 f)

Glacier
Dome
7142 m
(23,432 f)

Roc
Noir

7460 m
(24,215 f)

8091 m
26,545 f)

ANNAPURNA

Fluted
Peak

6645 m
(21,801 f)

The
Fang

7357 m
(24,137 f)

7647 m
(25,088 f)

South Annapurna Glacier

5670 m
(18,602 f)

5945 m
(19,514 f)

Tent
Peak

← Dhaulagiri
30 km
(18.5 m)

6316 m
(20,722 f)

7100 m
(23,294 f)

7150 m
(23,457 f)

Moditse

7219 m
(23,684 f)
Annapurna
South

Hiunchuli

6442 m
(21,135 f)

Overview map of Annapurna 1

II PASS

----------- FRENCH ROUTE 1950

—·—·— NORTHWEST ROUTE 1985

▲ MOUNTAIN

— — — SOUTHERN ROUTE 1970

░░░░░░░░ WEST ROUTE 1988

FIRST ASCENT OF ANNAPURNA 1950

Annapurna 1950.
What a goal!
What enthusiasm!
And what a team!

Maurice Herzog, although at the time not the strongest alpinist in France, was the driving force behind the expedition from the very start.

Lionel Terray belonged to the team—a war horse from Grenoble, a mountain guide in Chamonix, and constantly active, strong and willing to take risks. He was and remains one of the greatest mountaineers of our century. Together he and Lachenal formed a unique team, and it is right they were considered the French rope team of the postwar period.

This Louis Lachenal, who at the time was an instructor at the École Nationale de Ski et d'Alpinisme in Chamonix, was, it is true, a "foreigner" as far as the guides from Mont Blanc were concerned—he came from Annecy— but alongside Terray and Gaston Rébuffat, he ranked among the crème de la crème of young, up-and-coming postwar mountaineers in France.

Gaston Rébuffat, although born on the coast, was not only a mountaineer and author, he was one of the best and most determined climbers in Europe. He was "the master," who was later to become "the star."

The fine-limbed Jean Couzy, who at the age of twenty-seven was the youngest member of the team, was an airplane engineer by profession, and was not only a great climber but also a great character.

His climbing partner from Paris, Marcel Schatz, was built more solidly and was a gifted organizer. He was not a professional mountain guide, but was an enthusiastic alpinist who dedicated his entire holidays to the high mountains.

The team's cameraman was Marcel Ichac, a Himalaya veteran who had been on Hidden Peak, 26,469 feet (8068 m), as early as 1936 and had taken part in numerous expeditions. His experience was extremely useful, given that he knew a great deal about the problems encountered at high altitudes and about the help available locally. His contribution was of great importance for the young team.

The doctor, Jacques Oudot, a renowned surgeon, was a kind of life insurance policy for the expedition. He was to be the medicine man for the locals,

Maurice Herzog

and in the end the life saver for the exhausted, ailing team and, above all, for their expedition leader, Maurice Herzog.

With 6.6 tons (6 metric tons) of equipment, the expedition journeyed via India to Nepal, where they met their helpers, the Sherpas, "men of character and with a mind for great things," as Maurice Herzog writes in *Annapurna*. Later on, this expedition leader was accused of conducting himself like a colonial master, of behaving high-handedly and being nationalistic, and from time to time there were even doubts raised about Herzog and Lachenal's summit ascent. I talked to Gaston Rébuffat about this, and felt that even he resented Herzog to a certain extent, but I took this to be a feeling of jealousy—which is understandable. If one considers Herzog's success as an author and as a politician, then jealousy, even envy, in his milieu is only too easy to understand.

The more I researched the Annapurna Expedition and the older I grew, the clearer it became to me that the indisputable success on Annapurna in 1950 was due above all to Maurice Herzog. He had not only excelled as a mountaineer, but he had also achieved something unique with his life.

Annapurna 1950—what an expedition leader!

How was it on summit day?

Lachenal wanted to give up. It was too late. Past noon. He pushed for a descent. Herzog, however, would not consider retreating. He would have carried on alone to the summit. "I have lost all sense of time; it seems as if I have only been going for a few minutes," he felt, and drove his partner on. Onward, ever onward! Of course, the pair was confused because of the extent of the snowfields and the thin air. They had lost their sense of direction. But Herzog nevertheless wanted to continue upward; his goal was the summit. He did not think about the frostbite, the descent, or the narrowing time frame. Whether his insistence on making the ascent at any cost was right in mountaineering terms or not was immaterial to him. The summit was now his only target. I have had such feelings and also know well the impression that "the heavens were of sapphire blue."

Only because of Herzog's desire, because he could think of nothing else, did the two of them find enough strength to surmount the final hurdles. "Fortunately the snow is hard. By scraping our feet, and thanks to the crampons, we manage to gain enough purchase." One single wrong movement would have been disastrous! "We do not need to cut handholds, we drive in the ice ax as far ahead as possible and this serves as an anchor."

Thus, with their last reserves of willpower, the pair progressed. From time to time they looked up. Suddenly they saw a gully. Without quite knowing where it ended, one of them said, "Probably at the ridge." The summit ridge, Herzog hoped, and carried on climbing.

"We walked one behind the other, pausing after each step. Leaning on our ice axes, we tried to get our breath back and to calm our hearts, which were pounding fit to burst." How often I too have experienced precisely this kind of effort! And how many of the mountaineers who have climbed eight-thousanders know it from their own experiences! The last steps to the summit are usually nothing more than prolonged torture. Chest aching from the rapid breathing; throat, eyes, everything hurts; nose blocked; feet dead—and this hopelessness at the upper end of the world! Later on Maurice Herzog wrote about the state of humankind, just beneath the summit of an eight-thousander, capturing the mood precisely. He was the first to do this and it was authentic. He had no predecessors, neither summit conquerors nor authors, on this subject.

Only right at the top on the ridge did Herzog and Lachenal feel that they had almost reached their goal, and there was no longer anything that would hold them up. Herzog: "Neither of you needs first to look at the other's face in order to be convinced of his resolute determination." Thus they dragged themselves upward, one behind the other, as best they were able. Herzog again: "A small detour to the left, a few more steps...the summit ridge grows imperceptibly nearer. A few more rock boulders to go around." Then the wind beat toward them, fog billowed around in the south—they were on the

The summit ridge of Annapurna I

top, right on the top of Annapurna. More than 26,000 feet (8000 m) high.

Summit euphoria as described by Herzog, however, is not something I have come across. Herzog must have discovered this later. When we look back upon them, the pictures we have in our memories deceive us. The longing beforehand and the time we spend justifying afterward distort our memory. Thus Herzog created this description of the highlight of his life as a euphoric moment; it came from his desire to have experienced the greatest of summit hours, after so much commitment and such never-ending pain. The precise memory of the real situation quickly took flight.

"Our hearts overflowed with unspeakable happiness—our mission was accomplished. And at the same time something greater still had also been achieved. How beautiful life will now be!...The others! If only they knew!" Herzog rejoiced in his book about the short time he spent on the summit of the mountain. The fact that Herzog's summit report sounds a little overdramatic is by no means proof that he and Lachenal did not make it. The description of the summit area rings true: "The summit is a corniced crest of ice. The abyss on the other side is bottomless and terrifying. The walls drop down vertically beneath our feet."

Yes, that is precisely what it looks like from up there! Herzog's words are proof enough for me that the French were successful in 1950. And Lachenal never denied the summit ascent later on. One just had to imagine the situation: how exposed the pair of them were! Above them just empty space. "It is incomprehensible when you realize your ideals and your own potential so suddenly," Herzog wrote later, and that the feeling overcame him. He had never before felt such sheer joy.

Nearly 23,000 feet (7000 m) below, light clouds covered the Pokhara valley, the part of the world to which they had to return if they wanted to survive.

"Shall we go down?" Lachenal urged.

But something was still missing. Herzog wanted to take photos. In doing this, was he perhaps thinking about the proof of his success? A document for his later book? Or was this photography on the summit an inner necessity, matter of habit even?

"Hurry up!" Lachenal screamed.

Herzog fumbled feverishly in his rucksack, found the camera, then took out the little French pennant, which had gotten dirty in the rucksack, and tied it to the shaft of his ice ax. He now had to give the flag and "flagpole" to his companion in order to document the "victory." Lachenal was to stand there. Yes there, like that, with the little flag in his raised hand. But Lachenal just sat there, no victor's pose, no national pride, no flag in his hand. Herzog focused on Lachenal and pressed the shutter. As if in a trance, obeying an inner urge, he did what he had to do. The picture was out of focus but the second photo, the one of Herzog taken by Lachenal, would later be circulated the world over, billion-fold.

It was precisely with this photo of the victor's pose that critics wanted to question Herzog's credibility in 1950. With "Herzog on the summit," however, Lachenal's success was proven too! Fine, Lachenal is dead now, but if people want to argue about Herzog's success, then we are necessarily dealing with both the "summit men." Or did someone merely want to be part of Herzog's success of the century?

For me, there is no doubt; Herzog and Lachenal were right at the top. Of course Herzog wanted recognition and wanted to bring back proof of his victory from the summit. After all, he had not merely put together a pharmacy with Oudot—aspirin, sleeping tablets, amphetamines, a whole collection of preparations that were supposed to help get the French on the top of the first eight-thousander—he had invested his whole ambition in the Annapurna project. All the effort that went into the preparation, the choice of team, the best alpinists in the world, and his personal commitment were not to have been to no avail in the end. And for that reason too, he insisted upon a few summit pictures even at the limit of being sane.

One more thing: Herzog was not merely knowledgeable when it came to the literature written about the tragically failed expeditions on Nanga Parbat, "Kanch," and Mount Everest. In those days too, he jealously followed what the other mountaineers on the highest mountains in the world were doing, what they planned, and what they were searching for. He must have suspected how great the significance of the "first eight-thousander " would be in the mountaineering world.

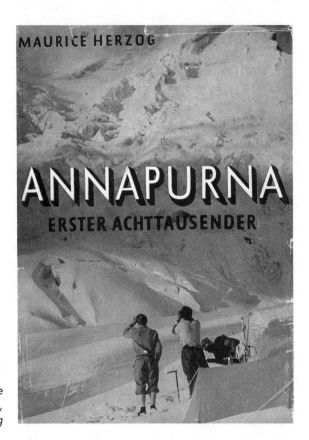

Cover of the worldwide bestseller Annapurna, *by Maurice Herzog*

But Herzog was not the only one who was ambitious and jealous; the others were ambitious and jealous too. Why else would alpinists act "so secretively from the start"? Herzog had spoken openly of his plans and he had still managed to be the first to climb an eight-thousander. He had not only taken responsibility for the ascent, he had remained the driving force behind it, right to the summit. More than all the others, he had been prepared to give it his all, to risk everything.

Now it was important to make the descent and return to France. At 26,545 feet (8091 m), his "victory" was worth nothing. Many others before him had reached the boldest possible of all goals and then died.

Once home, Herzog wrote, "It would have been ridiculous if two expeditions had been heading for the same summit at the same time." With that, he not only underlined the exclusiveness of his fame, he also defined his own style. He could not imagine how futuristic this statement would sound fifty years later. This makes clear that Maurice Herzog was not merely a creative and enthusiastic expedition leader, but also an extremely forward-looking man, who unfortunately only had one chance in his life to show what kind of mountaineer he really was.

I dare to make a very bold assertion here. Although the irrepressible Lionel Terray was there too, without Herzog the Annapurna Expedition of 1950 would have failed. And without his deeply shocking book about it, we would know less about the human state in the Death Zone. No, it is not the summit picture, but the frank description of their experiences on summit day and during the descent that prove that Lachenal and Herzog really were right at the top. The expedition leader and the mountain guide who stood together on the summit were closer than it may seem today.

Maurice Herzog, this expedition leader with a mind for "greatness" did not only write about himself in this connection. Herzog devised portraits of his expedition members that have remained consistent, character descriptions in which the pictures of those men who succeeded on great mountain tours after the Annapurna Expedition have remained vivid up to the present day. In spite of all the criticism about Herzog's expedition report, his Lachenal, his Rébuffat, his Couzy, and his Schatz have remained true to life. Although in the meantime all except Maurice Herzog have died, should we not grant the one remaining the recognition that he so rightly deserves? It is only right and fitting that Maurice Herzog should be given the title "Monsieur Annapurna."

Herzog needs no defense; he has found recognition worldwide. In spite of the many attempts that have been made to diminish his mountaineering and writing successes, fifty years after the first ascent of an eight-thousander the achievement and story of suffering of this leader and his character occupy a unique place in mountaineering history.

Annapurna I,
viewed from the
south

Even more than by the "summit victory," however, I am impressed by the "afterward"; how the crippled Herzog filled his life after the ascent of Annapurna, how he coped with the pain and the amputations is admirable. His life achievement, which certainly has its roots in the success on Annapurna, is not only great, it remains unique. The mountain cost him a lot, but it also gave him a lot. As he said himself, Annapurna showed him the right path. Only in the cold, fog, and storm did Herzog realize what he was capable of.

Therefore the ascent of Annapurna is and remains Herzog's own personal feat of heroism.

Unknown World

The story of the first ascent of Annapurna, told by Maurice Herzog using the expedition diaries—which were for the most part written by Marcel Ichac—and his own memories, is a mountaineering tale unlike any other. Perhaps one reason for this is that Louis Lachenal's personal diary and a great deal of information from the other members of the team were included, but above all because Herzog made a great effort to produce a true account, going beyond all glorification of the events.

Herzog's Annapurna book is the story of eight men in the Himalayas, a story I would like to retell here, on the one hand in order to acknowledge the pioneers' achievement, on the other hand in order to make clear just what it meant in 1950 to climb one of the fourteen peaks higher than 26,000 feet (8000 m), or eight-thousanders as they are called.

Let us look first at the equipment and supplies: 6 tons (6.6 metric tons) of material and provisions, but that is not very much if you consider that the expedition comprised eight men and was setting out for an unknown period of time into an unknown area in the Himalayas. Then there was the team—in a word, unique. Lucien Devies had succeeded in putting together the greatest talents of the day in one expedition. Maurice Herzog was to lead it. The Sherpa team too was excellent: "It would have been hard to find such a team in France," Ichac assures us. "Each individual gave a supreme performance; all movements were completely in tune with each other."

It is true that back home the French had dreamed of "transposing alpine mountaineering into the Himalayan context," but this tactical principal—their "Parisian Plans"—soon evaporated. In those days, it simply was not possible to have a super-lightweight approach to the ascent of a 26,000-foot (8000-m) peak, in spite of down and nylon; it would not have been a success.

When Herzog and his team saw the central Himalayas for the first time, they were both enthusiastic and disillusioned. Behind veils of cloud, enormous mountains towered up to the heavens. This spectacle exceeded all their

*Dhaulagiri I,
viewed from the
Miristi Khola*

expectations. Was this the impossible? "At first sight, we saw nothing other
than hazy cloud covering; yet when we looked more closely, we were able to
make out real ice walls at a great distance rising up to mighty heights above
the clouds and defining the horizon hundreds and hundreds of kilometers
away. To us, the shimmering wall seemed gigantic, immaculately compact,
with no cracks or gullies. Seven-thousanders lined up alongside the eight-
thousanders. We were overawed by the grandeur of this spectacle."

That was the Himalayas, and for months it had been the Holy Grail of
the French.

Then for the first time, doubts began to surface out of all this accumula-
tion of enthusiasm, doubts as to whether it would be possible to make any
progress up there, whether these mountains would simply prove too high.
But nobody voiced his fears openly. "We were all craning our necks to watch
the gigantic walls, which disappeared into the clouds in the blue sky 6000
meters (more than 19,000 feet) higher. The rocky sections were dark brown,
the snow shone dazzlingly. The light was so strong that we were forced to
blink," Herzog says.

The first impressions, and the mental state of the team, are described so
precisely in Herzog's book that the reader believes he or she is there with
them, as one of the pioneers.

On April 21 the approach march was over. Base camp was established in the gorge between Annapurna and Dhaulagiri. The French had taken only 14 days to cross Nepal from the south to the north. Now it was necessary to find a possible ascent route on one or another of the eight-thousanders.

First of all, the team reconnoitered the beautifully shaped Dhaulagiri, setting out from Tukucha in the Kali-Gandaki valley on several forays and in separate teams. But after only a few days, they had to admit that they were hopelessly on the wrong track. Herzog writes: "With the mountains here, it is clearly not such an easy task. The possibilities of ascent are very slim everywhere."

Merely to reach the foot of the steep flanks, the mountain proper, was a difficult and often dangerous undertaking. The trekking tourism that was to start twenty years later was not available in those days, nor were precise maps. The sketches showing the line of the ridge were imprecise or even wrong. Nor was there any advice available locally.

Slowly they realized that any Himalayan ascent required a kind of logistics different from that for a route in the Mont Blanc region: "Alpine technology is not sufficient here. Here you are forced to make an ascent in stages, constantly establishing new camps. Individual adventure must give way to collective enterprise." That was the summary when the different reconnoiter

The approach march to Annapurna I, with Dhaulagiri I in the background

View from Dhaulagiri I to Annapurna I

groups gave an account of how a mountain ascent could function in the Himalayas, what preparation was needed. It took a strong team, high-level camps, and a chain to furnish supplies if one wanted to have even the slightest chance of being able to climb mountains as high as Dhaulagiri or Annapurna.

Even Lionel Terray, who together with Louis Lachenal had made the second successful ascent of the North Face of the Eiger in 1947, and who was later to achieve world acclaim with the first ascent of Makalu in the Himalayas and of Fitz Roy in Patagonia, expressed disappointment after reconnoitering Dhaulagiri: "Not in any one single ascent in the Alps were we confronted by so many difficulties. People had never undertaken such acrobatic feats in the Himalayas."

I would like to dispute this last statement. In 1929 and 1931, Paul Bauer and his teams had achieved great things on the Northeast Spur of Kangchenjunga, and the English too had accomplished many bold things in the Himalayas in the period between the two wars, which still command my greatest admiration today. And when Terray maintained that "'Dhaula' will never be overcome," that was typical of this provocateur; like so many things that Terray reported as the irrefutable truth, it was said without thinking. In the meantime, it has been climbed hundreds of times.

Certainly, in 1950 Dhaulagiri would have been infinitely more difficult to climb than Annapurna; however, thirty-five years later, in 1985, the reverse would be true. After climbing Annapurna in April 1985, I managed to

The northern approach to Annapurna I is long, complicated, and dangerous.

climb from Tukucha nonstop to the summit of Dhaulagiri in 5 days in May of the same year, together with Hans Kammerlander, without any kind of "route preparation." We were completely alone on the mountain, and 2 days after reaching the summit we were back in the Kali-Gandaki valley. The difference was that we were able follow a known route and fall back on a tried and tested method. There were worlds between the French and us. Thirty-five years had passed. Knowledge and experience had multiplied. Above all, there was more equipment, and the equipment was lighter and better.

So what was known about the problems encountered at high altitude in 1950? Well, "during the ascent you suffer from the height, lack of oxygen, shortness of breath; during the descent, there is no trace of this; on the contrary, it is very easy," Herzog had hoped. This view is right and wrong at the same time, as the expedition would show. What the French recognized early on was not, however, enough to get to the top of Dhaulagiri.

Thus Herzog and his team turned to Annapurna, the foot of which they could reach using old shepherds trails and hunting paths. These were in part very difficult and exposed tracks—a real imposition on the porters—via which a lead team went on ahead to reach the cirque in the upper Miristi Khola. Everything had to be done very quickly now: reconnaissance, establishing the chain of camps, transport of equipment. The grinding hard work soon became too much for the team. Rébuffat no longer felt able to continue,

The north side, with the huge Sickle Glacier

Lachenal too had lost his appetite for the task, and for a short time even Terray lost his sense of humor and his famous desire to complain. Only Herzog, who in the beginning had spent more time in the valley than the others on account of his responsibility as expedition leader, continued to drive the Sherpas and sahibs forward, constantly going on ahead of them. He almost always climbed at the head of the party. Thus he not only acclimatized quickly, but was soon in top form and even managed to surpass himself. It was as if he knew that this ascent would be the greatest ascent, as he prepared himself for the "final assault" on the mountain that had become such a part of him that it had become "his" Annapurna.

The Big Climb

It was actually very late in the year—on May 31, when the monsoons might come any day—that Herzog and Lachenal packed their rucksacks for the summit ascent. But why Herzog and Lachenal in particular? This partnership had just evolved during the preparation phase. Herzog, who secretly packed a little French flag in his rucksack, was at that moment the strongest man in the team and had the motivation of an Olympic athlete. Not only in the Alps had Lachenal been Herzog's most frequent climbing partner, but he had helped him like no other with the establishment of the uppermost camp and had always looked out for his boss like a true mountain guide. Nevertheless, this was no client and guide relationship; Herzog and Lachenal complemented each other ideally. On only one matter were they not in

Only a few members of the 1950 French team had remained at the foot of the mountain when the "summit assault" began.

complete harmony: in their willingness to take risks. Lachenal would never have risked his life in the name of success. Herzog definitely would have done!

In these early June days in 1950, Herzog would have been prepared to risk anything. "We will climb up and only come down again when we have reached the summit," he said to one of his comrades. All or nothing was the name of this game, a game that he, at the head of the team, wanted to win and one that he would have lost in the end in spite of the interim victory on the summit had it not been for Terray, Couzy, Rébuffat, Schatz, and the Sherpas being there to lead the confused men back to the valley, and Oudot and Ichac to keep these exhausted invalids alive. Even so, the consequences were devastating.

The game of chance could begin.

This last ascent really did have something fateful about it.

Each team had its own job to do, and they all took up their positions. It was June 1, 1950.

Terray had worn himself out, although he had returned with Rébuffat the day before without setting up Camp V, because Rébuffat did not want to risk his feet becoming frostbitten; but Terray recovered quickly. He instinctively felt that the "great departure" was upon them, and made all the preparations for the summit ascent with the care that the others knew him for. Nevertheless he was now in second place on the starting grid. As the strongest mountaineer in the group, he would have been able to lead the second rope.

The morning of June 2 heralded a glorious day. The lower slopes of Annapurna were bustling with people. Terray and Rébuffat climbed with their Sherpas, Pansy and Aila, toward Camp III. Above this third camp, Schatz and Couzy, together with Sherpas Angawa and Fou-Tharkey, were in the process of traversing the great couloir. And beneath the Sickle Glacier, Herzog and Lachenal, together with Sherpas Ang-Tharkey and Sarki, tramped through the snow to the left. Above them towered the giant fractures of the sickle-shaped hanging glacier that cut off the world at the top.

Rébuffat and Terray, both in top form, climbed via Camp III, which they had reached at about 11:00 A.M. and dismantled, and pushed all the way up to Camp IV during the afternoon; in doing this, they hoped to gain a whole day. They had a lot to carry: two sets of high-altitude equipment, with fuel and more than 22 pounds (10 kg) of provisions. Couzy and Schatz were waiting for them at Camp IV.

In the meantime, Herzog and Lachenal had reached and extended Camp V. The storm tent was standing on a slightly sloping platform, which they had dug into the ice slope on the upper north flank with their ice axes. They were now hardly able to talk, let alone concentrate. Their conversation was stilted. And what an effort it was for them to make tea on the alcohol stove in the confined space of the tent! The summit aspirants took their "tablets" (probably stimulants; see Drugs and Doping in the chapter Critical View) with "military discipline." Yet it was impossible to eat anything. This last night before the "assault" was a long one and was made particularly horrendous for them because of the confined space, the headaches, and the shortness of breath. Then suddenly the storm came. The nylon tent flapped, the poles groaned. They both had to cope with the fear of being carried away by the wind, tent and all. With every gust, they grabbed hold of the poles. In their fear, they supported the tent from the inside. Later in the evening, it even began to snow.

Herzog and Lachenal lay half-dressed in their warm sleeping bags and listened to the gusts and the snow slides outside the tent. They had removed their boots and, icy as they were, stashed them inside their sleeping bags. Every minute was torture, every noise fueled their fear, each turn in their sleeping bags cost a lot of energy. Survival became a battle of will.

Lachenal, who lay on the valley side, slipped farther and farther toward the outside, hanging in the tent wall over the great abyss. Herzog was being pressed down by drifted snow on the side of the tent closest to the mountainside, and was finding it more and more difficult to breathe. Soon the two men stopped fighting against their miserable situation. They no

In 1950 dry snow lay on the névé slopes below the summit—just the cold and the snow, no life, no water, not even icicles.

longer counted the hours. They just suffered. When Herzog was hardly able to breathe, he turned and gasped for air. This just made the pressure worse. He began to give up. The weight of the snow pressed down upon him, and although he attempted to push against it with his arms in front of his chest, the difficulties remained. He continuously felt as if he were suffocating, and this was to remain so until the morning.

The other mountaineers in Camp IV experienced the storm as well. But thanks to aspirin, sleeping powder, and other medication, as well as the euphoric mood they had been in since the assault on the summit had started, they spent a satisfactory night. Only on the morning of June 3 did the storm gradually subside. At break of day, the wind let up completely.

In contrast, what an inhospitable place Camp V was! And in what a position both the mountaineers lay! They waited a long time for the first rays of the morning sun, but all was in vain. At half past five they could stand their position no longer and wanted to set off. But neither of them had the energy to make tea. So they continued dozing in the tent. Outside, in front of the tent, it would be more pleasant, not so confined and brighter, Herzog and Lachenal thought. So, up and away! Nevertheless, getting up was not easy. Every movement was like a contortion, each hand movement required great strength of will, every thought process took a great effort. Their thoughts were dulled. Herzog attempted to push back the icy mass that the cold and the night had thrown upon him. Again and again he pushed

Most mornings, the mists rise up the North Face of Annapurna from the Miristi Khola— the morning of June 3, 1950, was no exception.

his body against the center of the tent. Not a word was spoken. They found it so difficult to crawl out of their sleeping bags; it took forever. Then they needed to retrieve their totally frozen boots from the bottom of their sleeping bags and put them on. While doing this, the men kept being overcome with tiredness and collapsing. They were constantly out of breath, both had trouble tying their laces and gasped for breath again and again. Eventually Herzog was able to tie his gaiters; Lachenal was not. Even packing the rucksacks took a great deal of time and energy.

No, they wouldn't take a rope with them, and because the film camera was no longer working, they would leave that behind as well. It was all just ballast, just too heavy!

Only when the pair finally came out of the tent and put on their crampons did they begin to feel in any way human again. Yes, suddenly they were even confident. Herzog writes: "We are both dressed as warmly as possible, yet our rucksacks are light. We set off at six o'clock, happy to leave this awful place behind us. It is really good weather but cold too. The lightweight crampons dig deep into the very steeply inclined ice and snow surfaces, which we have to climb first." It all sounds very matter of fact, too banal for a mountaineer. But in addition we have to imagine where they were, how they were moving and at what altitude, and how exposed it all was!

Soon the slope grew easier-angled, the snow crusty. Where it held, it was quite easy going, but every now and then the men sank into the soft powder

The narrow ridge between the South Face and the North Flank, the knife edge between life and death, was like an alien world for Herzog.

snow, and this made progress very difficult. More and more frequently they stopped to breathe, to look around. They stood and stared and gasped for breath. Without thinking. Without speaking a word to each other. They took it in turns to go first and break trail through the snow. It was hellishly hard work taking the lead. Each of them was freezing cold and each of them was encapsulated in his own inner world, only looking ahead as far as the next few paces.

As the horizon unfolded, so their world diminished in size. No, that is no contradiction; it comes from the lack of blood in the head. Thus it was that they gradually stopped assessing their situation, stopped thinking. Their capacity for thought had diminished to such an extent that they were no longer able to distinguish between apathy and exhaustion. Although they were both aware of their weakened mental state, neither one of them had a sensible thought. Only Lachenal frequently thought about giving up. But Herzog wanted to continue. To the summit! It was more comfortable to think this one thought than to force themselves to imagine where they were, where they were going, and how they would get back to the others. Herzog's only impulse was directed upward.

Even in their special padded clothing, Herzog and Lachenal were not immune to dying of hypothermia, and each time they stopped, they stamped their feet hard to ward off the cold. Once Lachenal even removed a boot because he was afraid that his feet might be frostbitten; nothing—not Annapurna, not even the honor of France—were worth the risk of frostbite. He had no wish to lose even the little toe on his left foot. Maurice Herzog was different. He was pushy, he wanted to carry on and was prepared to take any kind of risk.

Each step was now an effort. They carried on, two steps at a time, until they were exhausted, then they had to stop and rest. Onward! So it went from rest to rest. Lachenal began to doubt whether they had already gone too far.

"Freezing your feet off...is that what it's all about, do you think?" he asked Herzog.

And what was all this hesitation about? Herzog knew precisely that this danger existed, but he was tormented less by the specter of frostbite than by the doubts as to whether they would reach the summit. Without success, there was no return for him, not anymore.

Today we might well ask ourselves whether the prize of Annapurna outweighed such a high risk. Herzog did not ask himself this; he just wanted to get to the top.

During these hours, Marcel Ichac followed the movements on the mountain from Camp II using binoculars, noting how the operation was proceeding. This is one extract from his expedition diary: "On June 3, Oudot, together with three Sherpas, climbed up toward Camp II." Then through the binoculars he observed two ropes above the icefalls, to the left of the sickle, "Terray and Rébuffat and, behind them, Couzy and Schatz." At first he could see nothing of Herzog and Lachenal. In the meantime, clouds and fog had come up between him and the summit team. There were hardly any breaks in the clouds to make it possible for him to follow the events as they unfolded, and the uppermost slopes, which were less steep, could not be seen from below anyway.

The wind swept the spindrift around, and the summit area of Annapurna was completely swathed in swirling gray snow.

In spite of his mental state, Maurice Herzog still knew enough to be aware that in the "final stage, when approaching the summit, it is impossible to avoid using a great deal of strength: for then the physical and psychological potential of each of us releases his entire energy, with only a little regard for conserving the necessary energy for the descent." While planning the climb, he had repeatedly imagined this situation, so that in spite of shortness of breath, apathy, and cold, he was able to endure the fear and hopelessness. It was now solely a question of mental strength, of continuing due to strength of will and of identifying with the goal he had before him.

Herzog looked at Lachenal, who now seemed like a ghost to him.

The beautifully shaped Machapuchare, a holy mountain, to the south of Annapurna I

Meanwhile, Lachenal presumed Herzog to be a madman. Each of them was now living merely for himself, climbing for himself. Remarkably, the physical effort diminished; both men were beside themselves. Hours earlier and lower down, everything had surely been much harder. "Is it the drugs taking effect, or is it hope that now gives us wings? " Herzog asked himself.

Lachenal suddenly stopped and asked, "If I turn back now—what will you do?" Said flippantly in reply to Herzog's euphoria, it had to sound like an insult. Herzog hesitated and then, in his mind's eye as if in a film, he saw pictures from the past flash before him, "the days of the approach march in the blazing heat, the painstaking ascents, each individual's enormous effort in the fight for the mountain, the daily heroism shown by my companions in establishing and dismantling the camps. And now we are nearly there! In one, possibly two, hours we might have achieved it! And now we are supposed to give up?" Never! With success so close, there could be no turning back now.

Impossible! Herzog knew even in his deepest subconscious what the stakes were. He had made the decision, he had absolutely resolved to carry on, to get to the summit. For that, no sacrifice was too big for him. All or nothing— yes, he would even have carried on alone.

"I'll carry on alone!" he said without hesitation to Lachenal, defiantly, and then, certain that he would follow, "Go on then, if you want to turn back. I'm climbing to the summit."

"Then I'll come with you!" Lachenal had no other choice.

Lachenal's spontaneous reply tells us a lot about the mountain guide's sense of responsibility and even more about his sense of loyalty to an expedition comrade. It was not simply Herzog's declaration of intent that drove Lachenal on, it was much more the instinct of the experienced mountain guide, which meant he would go along although he saw the immediate dangers more clearly than his companion, who was blinded by his desire to get to the summit. With altitude sickness, greedy for the mountain and blinded by ambition, Herzog carried on.

Thus it was that Herzog and Lachenal made it to the top. For me, there is no doubt that they were up there. The way in which Herzog describes the summit hours proves, more than all the photographic evidence, that they reached the highest point. For right up there in the Death Zone where reason stops functioning, Herzog imagined himself upon a mountain that he only dreamed about. "A joy without compare" filled him in this place so close to the heavens, and filled him too with pride in the risks he had taken. At the same time, he was far removed from the ability to recognize where he actually was: "An enormous gulf separates me from the rest of the world. I am in another kingdom, deserted and barren, lifeless, frozen stiff in the cold. In a fantastic kingdom, where man does not belong....The way in which I view my companions and my surroundings has something unreal about it...within me I am forced to smile at our pitiful efforts. At the same time I am observing all my movements from outside. Yet they are no longer an effort; it is as if gravity has been removed."

Suddenly they were standing high up on this eight-thousander, on the slightly inclined summit ridge. The summit of Annapurna is nothing but a snow dome, banal but very exposed. The strong wind made them feel insecure and, looking down over the South Face, even Lachenal was gripped by horror. The surrounding mountains—Machapuchare, Dhaulagiri, Manaslu—they were hardly aware of them. A bottomless world!

Just one more photo, the obligatory summit photo had to be taken! Lachenal achieved what Herzog no longer was capable of, the summit photo taken more from the north side. Then they began the descent. It was like an escape. Lachenal was on the move right after the last summit photo was taken, he wanted to get back—his toes! He was afraid. In his panic, he was no longer a mountain guide, he just climbed down. Herzog: "I am hurrying as fast as I possibly can, but the terrain is dangerous. And fearful with every step that the weight of one's body in this snow might trigger an avalanche. Lachenal is already on the great diagonal traverse. He is moving at a speed that I would not have thought him capable of. Now I too have to cross this zone where rock and snow are intermingled. Finally I am beneath the wall. I really hurried and am completely out of breath. I take off my rucksack, take off my gloves." Herzog no longer knew why he had wanted this break, and

After a new fall of snow and in the mist, the deeply crevassed North Face of Annapurna I is dangerous, particularly for an exhausted team making their descent.

his gloves had already slipped off. He watched them racing down the slopes. They disappeared into the depths, were immediately out of reach. He saw them racing down the slope.

That was the start of a life of suffering, one that an outsider can hardly imagine.

No Sense of Direction

All Herzog now wanted was to get down to Camp V, where he expected help and rescue. Rébuffat and Terray would be there, he thought. Now, after the summit, in his hour of need they were his mainstay. Just as hours before he had wanted nothing other than to get to the summit, now he just climbed downward, without gloves, stumbling and half crazy. "Not for one moment did I think to take the socks out of my rucksack, the ones that I always have with me for situations like this; I just set off and attempted to catch up to Lachenal."

It had been two o'clock in the afternoon when the pair had reached the summit; they had been on the go since they set off at 6:00 A.M.

Herzog had lost all sense of time. He imagined he was running and would soon reach safety. In reality he swayed and staggered very slowly downward, as if in a trance, with freezing limbs. Again and again he had to stop to catch his breath, and to get his bearings. Where was he, where was Lachenal, where to next? Clouds in the sky, everything overcast, dirty gray, misty fog everywhere. How difficult it had become all of a sudden to get one's bearings! Onward! In the icy wind of the storm, Herzog stumbled onward. He had to catch up to his partner.

"Biscante!" Herzog used Lachenal's nickname to call after him.

Where was he? Suddenly, 650 feet (200 m) farther on, Herzog saw a figure.

"Biscante!"

But the figure moved on like an animal, not pausing for even a moment.

When Herzog reached Camp V, he was suffering from hypothermia, confused and exhausted. His whole body was shaking. Crazy and confused, he first threw his arms around Terray. He was only able to say that they had been on the top, on the summit, and how happy he was. "What kind of happiness was this?" Terray asked himself, with these hands, this glazed expression, this stuttering voice?

It was only later that they found Lachenal; he too was confused. He must have fallen. Lying in the snow beneath the camp, he did not want to climb back up to Camp V; he just wanted to carry on climbing down. Terray forced him to come to the camp, to climb up and to stay there for the time being. It would soon be night, and in addition, the storm was getting worse and worse.

By now, Herzog was completely apathetic. He looked dreadful. Rébuffat massaged his fingers and then his feet, which were transparent and thickly swollen. Terray worked on Lachenal's feet in the other tent. The dramatic part of the expedition had begun.

Outside the storm howled around the tents, growing louder and louder. Then there was the mist and the night. Everything had become uncertain. There was cold and snow everywhere, both outside and inside. It was snowing. Again and again, the storm threatened to tear away the tents. With every gust of wind, the men feared they might have to die there in that cold, dark place.

There were only two air mattresses left in the camp. Herzog and Lachenal were lying on them, while their caregivers sat on ropes, rucksacks, and provisions sacks. In order not to lie on the snow, they put up with numb legs, pressure points, and all sorts of contortions—and, in addition to this, the cold. It was too much pain. They could not even begin to think about sleeping.

From time to time the injured men cried out in fear or because they were thirsty. Only Terray still had the energy to prepare something hot to drink. When he had finished, he informed Rébuffat in the second tent that he should come and fetch a beaker full for himself and Herzog. The hot liquid did Herzog good, and for a short time he felt better. If only he had been able to drink more!

It was during this night that Herzog's existence became a living hell. He fantasized about dying as the violent gusts of wind raged on. It continued snowing, and the weight of the snow pressed down more and more on the roof of the tent. Fear of being suffocated added to his woes.

In the early morning, Herzog heard voices. Were they coming from the other tent? Where was he? Terray was there, massaging Lachenal's feet over and over again. Again and again he gave him hot drinks. How good that was! Rébuffat, who by now was dead tired, was pleased when he felt that a little warmth had returned to Herzog's limbs. The expedition leader seemed far away, already half unconscious, as day broke. He hardly noticed how the hours passed. He was lucky not to realize how dramatic the situation was. He just groaned away to himself, by now half awake. In a kind of drugged stupor, he accepted his fate. Because of the great weight of the heavy snow on the tent, he also had the terrible feeling of slowly suffocating. He turned a little, struggled for breath, and dozed again. All in vain; the pressure did not ease off.

"Come on, we have to get away from here!"

Was that someone calling? When Terray called again, "We have to set off!" Herzog was already half dead. He heard the sounds without understanding what they meant.

"Was it morning already?" Herzog asked himself. The storm was still holding its own. Was this now the monsoon?

Rébuffat made an effort to sit his apathetic tent companion upright, but Herzog just kept on keeling over sideways, as if he was dead. He was sitting there as helpless as a baby, and Rébuffat had to put his boots on for him to get him ready for the descent. Meanwhile, Terray was dressing Lachenal. His feet were by now so swollen that they would not fit in his own boots. What could be done? Terray quickly made the decision to give him his, which were larger. But in order for him to be able to put on Lachenal's boots, he had to cut out the leather at the front so that his toes poked out. Then he put a sleeping bag and some provisions in his rucksack and called to tell Rébuffat to do the same.

But either Terray's words could not be understood, or they were lost in the storm; in any case, it was chaos. Impatience, fear, and aggression all surfaced. Even helplessness. Each of them wanted to leave this hell behind them as quickly as possible, but nobody knew how.

Lachenal and Terray had been ready for ages, while Rébuffat was still taking care of Herzog. The others were standing outside and stamping their feet. "Hurry up!" they called.

"We're going!" Terray said suddenly. It sounded like a threat. Herzog and Rébuffat finally crawled out of their tent, but there were only two ice axes for four people. Rébuffat and Terray took them for themselves and pushed the invalids onward. Terray led Lachenal and Rébuffat took Herzog on his rope. Both tents remained behind.

When the roped parties went out into the gusts of snow and started the descent, they immediately lost all sense of direction. No visibility; the ground was flowing beneath them; with the wind blowing hard, they could not even hear as far as 6½ feet (2 m) away. Much later, the wind calmed down, but the fog remained and snow was falling in large, thick flakes. Where was the continuation route? They looked around. They stared at the nothingness.

The four carried on, in single file: Lachenal first, followed by Terray, then Herzog, and Rébuffat last. It is impossible to describe the feeling of having lost all sense of direction in a whiteout. You stumble into it and keep on falling. The distances are deceptive, the elevations turn out to be dips.

Surrounded by fog and snowflakes, the glacier surface beneath them like an abyss, and everything blending into a single bright, contourless cage. It was impossible to tell hollows from humps, cracks from seracs. Which way was up? The shadows of the ice storm took on fantastic shapes. They appeared to move and grow before their eyes and then to disappear into nothingness when they had gone past them. How quickly nature was able to make fools out of the best mountaineers in the world!

Without intending to, the four men looked for outlines as they descended, but again and again they only discovered one of their own party. Otherwise, there was nothing.

These four ghostly figues—crusted in snow, swaying, searching—were not yet so despairing that they would have given up completely. They did not even know how lost they really were. Yes, they just had to keep on going down, down, down. To the left! Past an ice boulder! Down! But what was down? What was left, what was right? They sank down farther and farther into the soft snow, paused frequently. These crazy wanderings were not only enough to drive them to the brink of despair, they were a major effort for completely exhausted men.

Rébuffat and Terray looked at each other searchingly. Were they too high? Too low? Neither of them knew how to voice it. Frequently they were unable to carry on in the soft snow, so they turned back and tried again. Once they climbed to the upper edge of an ice cliff, where they suspected they would find the only correct passage down onto the lower steep slopes. Rébuffat was now in the lead; as routefinder, he was responsible for finding the shortest way out. But what was responsibility now? And why were they in such a wretched situation?

Herzog was determined to carry on to his death, so they had to rescue him. He followed Rébuffat without saying a word. The leaders could not find the key passage back to Camp IV; they frequently went wrong and experienced one disappointment after another. In addition, the fear of ending up in the darkness or in an avalanche was increasing. Hour by hour, the snow covering grew thicker. Undaunted, Terray and Rébuffat just kept on going.

Like machines they dug their way through the snow, taking turns at breaking trail. Silently, and without delay, they continued on down.

What a performance it was! The natural strength of these men, who were such good mountaineers and who were so different in character, had never been seen so clearly as in this time of need. Here was Rébuffat's persistence: the toughness that would make him famous. He never gave up, pushing his way through the snow with unbelievable strength of will, until he collapsed exhausted. What a desperate situation, and what an effort! His progress often could only be measured in inches (centimeters).

Perhaps Rébuffat did not give up because he knew that they would all die if he did not try everything. He had to bring the others down to safety! It was a case of summoning up the last reserves of strength and nevertheless carrying on for days. He did not want to die.

Terray was different. This strong man charged about first of all; then, as if blind, he raced like a madman into this world of fog, collapsed and stood up again, confused and disoriented. Terray was a natural phenomenon, gesticulating wildly in the fog as if he wanted to tear down the walls of the prison in which they were trapped. His strength and his determination were enormous, yet in this situation he too was powerless.

The sick Lachenal called Rébuffat a fool and crouched down in the snow. But were these malicious remarks the words of a man who was still sane? He wanted to dig a hole in the snow and wait for better weather. He continued to make derogatory remarks about Terray and the others as being failures. In spite of all this, Terray continued to drag Lachenal along behind him, paying him no attention. He held him on the rope, talked to him, first reassuringly and then barking commands, speaking as if to an animal. And Lachenal obeyed. As if he were forced to do what Terray did, he trotted along behind him.

In the meantime, this wretched pile of bodies had become completely lost. Only a miracle would now save the four men.

The Never-Ending Descent

Presently, Terray, Rébuffat, Lachenal, and Herzog were sitting in the whiteout. Stuck. Where precisely were they? Somewhere on the North Face of Annapurna, yes, but where exactly? Their cries for help were in vain. Nothing! No answer. Their clothes were frozen stiff, their hands and feet began to freeze again, and the time was quickly passing, much too quickly now. Soon it would be evening again. This helplessness!

In spite of their great fear, none of them complained. Perhaps they were at odds among themselves, and each one with himself. Nobody reproached the others, not now, not anymore. When the night suddenly arrived, the decision was made to dig a hollow as Lachenal had suggested. Now they had no other option. If they were to spend the night on the slopes in the open air, they would die. Torn away by the wind or frozen to death before the morning came.

I know what it means to bivouac out in the open at a height of over 23,000 feet (7000 m) without protection—it is terrible. In their condition, it would certainly have been fatal.

While Terray began to dig the hollow with an ice ax, a few steps farther on, Lachenal disappeared with a cry. He had obviously fallen into a glacier crevasse, broken through the crust and disappeared. Vanished without a trace. Terray called into the abyss. From the hole into which Lachenal had fallen came only the icy breath of the glacier. Fortunately, he was roped up.

"Lachenal!"

No reply. Terry gave the rope a few mighty tugs.

"Come on down!" Lachenal now replied.

"Down to you?"

"Yes!"

"Are you injured?"

"I'm OK and it will be better to spend the night here!"

"Better than where?"

"Better than up there."

Without hesitating, Terray let himself slide into the hole. Via a toboggan slide—one about 32 feet (10 m) long—he shot down into the crevasse that opened out down below. Then Herzog followed. A tug on the rope informed Rébuffat that he should follow. The journey down was no luxury, but it was protected from avalanches and initially the cold in the icy interior was bearable. Later on Herzog said: "All of us together would never have had the strength to dig a hole in the ice large enough to protect us from the wind outside."

The first miracle had happened: By chance they had stumbled upon a place to spend the night. How did they set about organizing themselves in the darkness? They didn't! They just crouched in the snow, with the ice all around them. All of it had nothing to do with romance. The space was very confined, new snow pattered down on them from above. First they took off their boots, otherwise their restricted feet would have frozen. Although the temperature in the ice cave was almost constant, they were soon terribly cold. In addition there was the damp, the snow, the darkness it was unbearable.

In spite of the lack of space, Terray still massaged Lachenal's feet from time to time. He was now sharing his sleeping bag with him. The pair of them squeezed up close together in order to warm each other and to keep themselves alive. Rébuffat, whose feet had frozen solid, massaged his own feet. Herzog remained motionless the whole time; as if he had sunk into a half sleep, he just lay there and tried to doze. He was apathetic and silent.

The 45-degree snowslopes beyond the North Buttress of Annapurna I, which drops diagonally from the summit into a huge glacial basin. After a fresh fall of snow, these slopes become an avalanche chute.

Nobody spoke. "We each retreated into our own little world," Herzog remembers later when thinking about this night.

Herzog's hands and feet continued to get more and more frostbitten. What could he do to prevent it? He just huddled himself together and in his hopelessness forgot about the passage of time until the cold drove him to unconsciousness.

When Terray realized that Herzog had given himself up for lost, he massaged him for almost two hours. That alone could not save Herzog but it did at least give him mental strength. Terray was his guardian angel and Herzog admired him: "If he is prepared to help me, then it would be ungrateful of me not to want to live," thought Herzog. He later recognized that this feeling had helped him make it through the night. So he pulled himself together.

When Herzog describes this night and his condition, we can quite believe his resignation. It was the beginning of death. "I am not suffering, and this surprises me. My heart seems completely frozen. It is as if everything material has dropped away. I seem to be wide-awake, yet I am suspended in a kind of peaceful happiness. A weak breath of life is still within me, but this is growing weaker by the hour. I no longer react to Terray's efforts. This is nearing the end, I think. Is this cave here not the most beautiful grave? I am not finding it difficult to die, I feel no regret, I smile at the thought."

As day gradually dawned, they all awoke from their numbness, even Herzog. So he was still alive. Amazed that they were still able to see the day from the inside of the mountain, Herzog in his apathy remained lying down longer than the others. Terray, Rébuffat, and Lachenal began to right themselves. Herzog heard Rébuffat say, "It's still too early to set off." With eyes half open he saw shadows next to him and saw it begin to grow dark in the grotto. Ugly gray. There were individual heads, bodies, and a constant hissing noise. Suddenly everything went completely black and the snow started to pour in, more and more snow. They all shook themselves. Would their cave be filled in?

They could no longer see anything and could hardly breathe. Outside there was obviously an avalanche from all the newly fallen snow. The powder snow swept over them like a torrent of water. The air inside the cave was full of swirling spindrift and the snow crystals penetrated everything, their noses, their clothes, their lungs. All four of them instinctively bent forward, kept their heads down, and protected their faces with their arms. But snow and even more snow forced its way into their mouths, ears, and noses. It soon filled every orifice. A long time passed until finally the pressure subsided and the snowfall grew lighter.

After the fear had subsided and the damp snow been plucked from faces and necks, the hustle and bustle started. Lachenal was the first to find a pair of boots and wanted to get out. When he tried to put them on, they were too small. They weren't his or, rather, they were not Terray's boots, they were Rébuffat's. Thus Rébuffat was the first to scramble up the toboggan slide and into the open air.

"What's the weather like?" he heard Terray's voice calling from the depths.

"It's windy but you can't see anything."

"Nothing?"

"No, nothing at all."

The others were still digging around for their equipment. Lachenal and Herzog were searching around the floor of the glacier crevasse for their boots. They found crampons, an ice ax, but no boots. They could not find their boots! So Lachenal climbed up the rope without boots and once he was outside he realized that the sky was blue. He ran about like a madman, shouting, "It's beautiful! It's beautiful!"

But once at the top of the chute, Terray too saw almost nothing. Like Rébuffat, he too was snow-blind. Was Lachenal now the last hope of rescue? Yes, he now had to help the three of them, being the only invalid without visual impairment, for the others were worse off than he was.

Herzog continued to be numbly indifferent to everything. He must have given up all hope. With his bare hands and feet, he dug his way through the snow on all fours. Like a mole he worked away at the floor of the crevasse until he at last found his and Lachenal's boots. The descent could now begin, but Herzog mumbled, "This is the end. We're lost."

"Why?" asked Terray.

Herzog replied, "We can't get out of here anymore."

Yet Herzog, who was still in the crevasse with the boots in his hands, without knowing what was going on the outside still did not give up. But his first collapse of the day happened as he climbed out of the glacier crevasse. He thought he was going to die. Then he fell again and just continued dragging himself along on all fours. Lachenal at first wanted to descend even barefoot. But the snow-blind Terray forced him to sit down in order to be able to put his boots on. Which of the four mountaineers was now the least mad?

It was a sorry picture, the way the four invalids prepared themselves for the descent. Rébuffat and Terray were snow-blind and so those with wounded feet, Lachenal and Herzog, had to guide the visually impaired. At the same time, the weather was glorious. A large amount of fresh snow lay on the slopes, the mountains gleamed.

Once again Herzog wanted to remain behind and die. He was completely apathetic and felt as if he were far away from the others, as if on another star. Did he know that he would die anyway, or was it just that he no longer wanted to be a burden to his friends? Later on he wrote about this: "Next to the others I am living as if in a dream. My end is near, I can feel it, yet it is the kind of end that any alpinist would wish for in harmony with the passion that has been his life's inspiration. With wide-open senses, I am thankful to the mountains for showing themselves to me today in the entirety of their beauty. For me their silence is like the peace of a church. I am not suffering, nor do I feel the remotest fear. My calm is horrifying."

Herzog now lay in the snow, gasping for breath, without boots, without strength. Then Terray came up to him and forced him to stand up. "We are all going to make it back!" he shouted at him. All or none was now the motto. That was an order.

In the meantime, Terray had cut open the uppers of his old boots with his penknife so that Herzog could slip them on. Now that they were slit open, he was able to put on the boots.

So suddenly Terray, snow-blind Terray, was once again the driving force. Nobody dared to oppose him. He ranted and shouted.

Finally all four of them were ready to set off. Yet at the start they could hardly move, with their stiff joints, and only Lachenal was in a position to see, to find the way, to guide. But Lachenal too had no longer any idea what he was doing. He looked completely worn-out, helpless, drained. He glanced around, his eyes confused. He constantly wanted to move on, in the wrong direction, to go straight down.

Nothing could be done from Advanced Base Camp to help the casualties high on the mountain; only certain parts of the torturous route were visible from below.

In the lower camps, of course, everyone—the Sherpas, Oudot the doctor, Marcel Ichac—was concerned about the four lost friends but that was no use to them up there. They had first to help themselves, before they could hope for help from below. On June 5 at the Advanced Base Camp, the waiting expedition members were thinking about what was to be done. Were they perhaps the only survivors of the eight-man team?

Finally on this June 5 the Sherpas Sarki, Aila, Ang-Tharkey, and Pansy as well as Couzy and Schatz finally got close to these madmen wandering around lost among the icefalls. When the two little groups were within shouting distance, Schatz took the initiative. Painstakingly he worked his way up to Terray, who was still back at the bivouac site of the crevasse camp as if he needed to protect something. Schatz made the sudden decision to search about in the snow in the crevasse, where the camera and Herzog's ice ax remained. Only then did Schatz, who of course wanted to be last, secure the ropes at the bottom. Once again they had a guide, a sahib who was master of the situation.

After a short time, however, the first rope, Rébuffat and Herzog, were again caught by a new snow avalanche. In fact all morning Herzog had sensed this danger through all the pores in his skin, but had been neither competent nor strong enough to warn them about it. He was a wreck, no longer a leader. "There was vibration in the air and this warmth, masses of snow everywhere, just waiting to be set in motion.

"In Europe one cannot even imagine the avalanches here. They cannot

Avalanches are a daily occurrence on the North Face of Annapurna I, particularly after snowfalls.

even be compared with the avalanches in our own Alps. They crash down in a kilometer-wide front and a storm that sweeps away everything in its path rages ahead of them."

As Herzog had feared, the slope on which they had been standing had started to move: "Suddenly this snow covering is ripped out from beneath the Sherpas' feet; the crack becomes longer and wider. A sudden crazy idea comes to my mind: I should run up the slope to reach firm ground!" But it was impossible in his situation. It was all too late! Herzog had already been lifted up off his feet by the superhuman force and carried away. The Sherpas disappeared before his very eyes into the depths.

"I do a somersault and see nothing more. My head crashes against the ice. In spite of all my efforts I cannot breathe. A hefty bump on my left thigh is terribly painful. I turn a cartwheel like a jumping jack....Through the snow pushing past my eyes, the dazzling brightness of the sun hits me like a bolt of lightning. The rope, which is holding Sarki, Aila, and me together, wraps itself around my neck!"

Herzog assumed that this was his end and that the Sherpas who had been dragged down the slope ahead of him were about to strangle him.

"The pain is unbearable—I'm suffocating. Again and again I hit the ice, I am spun from one ice boulder to another. The snow is crushing me to death. With a sudden jolt the rope that is tangled around my neck tautens and holds me tight. Before I come to my senses I begin to urinate involuntarily and violently."

When Herzog opened his eyes, everything had been turned on its head.

"I am hanging upside down; the rope holds me by the throat and is wrapped around my left leg. I am held in a kind of trap, swaying over the shining ice, poised above the abyss. I spread out my elbow to the walls in an attempt to halt the unbearable swinging motion, which is pulling me from one side to the other. Beneath me I can make out the last steep steps of the great couloir. I start to breathe again and I bless the rope, which in spite of this fall has held."

In this emergency situation Herzog began to fight again: "I have to try to free myself from this situation. My hands and feet have lost all sense of feeling, yet these small cracks in the wall offer me help. They are just big enough for me to shove the rand of the boot sole into them at least. By shaking myself repeatedly I manage to get the rope off from around my left leg. With a great effort I am able to gain a hold here and there, and then to climb up a few meters. After each movement, I pause and feel that I have exhausted my last physical strength. I may have to let go at any moment."

No, Herzog did not let go; he did not even release his grasp until he had been freed, rescued from this desperate situation. Yes, rescued, as if by a second miracle! The party had been carried 500 feet (150 m) by the avalanche and nobody had perished.

"Another desperate effort and I gained another couple of centimeters! I pull on the rope and feel something soft at the other end, the bodies of the Sherpas. I call—but how faint it sounds. Deathly silence all around."

Presently, Herzog became unconscious. The light went out. As if a gloomy cloud were drawing over him he sank into unconsciousness. Later he saw the shocked faces of Aila and Sarki at the edge of the ice above him. Above them only the clear blue sky. The Sherpas pulled him up and in doing so gave him back his life strength and safety, and above all a little bit of courage to carrying on living after this brush with death.

As if by a miracle, the rope had hung itself around an ice boulder. Suddenly Rébuffat appeared as well. They were still all there and, as if by divine intervention, none of them had been injured.

It was still a very long way to the plateau of Camp II. Herzog was not only suffering because of his frostbite, he was at the end of his strength. More and more often, he just wanted to stop and sit down. He would have liked to give up more than anything.

"Why carry on? For me everything is now over. I have a clear conscience."

Perhaps the others at least could be saved if he were to remain behind. Of course, the responsibility—he was prepared to shoulder the responsibility for their current situation. So he dragged himself and his burden of responsibility on down the mountain without complaining.

When Herzog saw the tents of Camp II, he once again drew upon all his

Across avalanche-prone slopes, through labyrinthine crevasse systems, and wading the whole time through deep snow, the Annapurna team made its way slowly back to Advanced Base Camp.

reserves of strength in order to walk upright, to make progress. He was peacefully resigned to accepting his fate. Only in order to fulfill his mission did he carry on, although all he really wanted to do was sleep. His ambition on the summit was enough to make you despair, his helplessness now enough to make you cry. But it was too late now for any regrets.

It was this sacrifice that had led to success and it was this capacity for suffering that kept Lachenal, Terray, Herzog, and Rébuffat going now. Torturously Herzog crawled, stumbled, and walked down the slope. He rappelled whenever possible, and crawled over the ice boulders. Scraps of his skin were often left behind on the rope and on the ice. His right arm was stiff right up to and beyond his elbow. There were spatters of blood everywhere. No, it was no longer a descent, it was the decline and fall of a victorious expedition.

What a miserable sight this team was now, not a pretty sight, all these old faces!

Herzog did not expect sympathy, but merely wished for an end to his suffering. He was still observing as if from outside the situation in which they found themselves, and his own personal misery. At the same time, he analyzed everything precisely. "My hands are in a terrible state. I feel as if the flesh is peeling away from the bones."

From below the Sherpas were now climbing up toward the returning ones. And now the tents of Camp II could not only be seen, they took on color as well. There were people there too, and this gave Herzog renewed courage.

Every dashed hope is soon forgotten when help is at hand. It is true

Herzog took each step as if it were his last, and each breath was torture, but at the same time each yard (meter) they gained on the descent to the tents was like a resurrection.

When they finally reached Camp II—Ichac and Oudot ran toward the returning climbers—Herzog could not wait to throw his arms around his friends and to announce the victory. He called loudly to them all: "We are returning from Annapurna! The day before yesterday we were up there, Lachenal and I!"

Rébuffat immediately withdrew into a tent, as if he was unable to stand so many contradictions. The hero was now Herzog, and he alone.

It is certainly fascinating how this man believed in the summit and how his success on the mountain helped him to get down, but it is equally disturbing how he fooled himself again and again over his "news of victory." Was this the only reason he needed to tell everyone about the victory? And is this perhaps why today there is still so much lack of understanding for his "Hero's Story"?

Was this outbreak of pride in the safety of the camp perhaps a result of his close encounter with death? Yes, in all his pain, in his efforts that had far exceeded the normal human capacity, this return was like a rebirth for Herzog; each new breath was the real "victory." The real highlight in mountaineering is always coming down, the returning "from another star" back to the human world.

As the second group neared the camp, with Lionel Terray in the lead, guided by a porter, there were deeply distressing scenes. Almost blind as Terray was, he supported himself on Ang-Tharkey and walked along stooped like an invalid. Painstakingly, the strongest man of the expedition dragged himself toward the safety of the camp, confused and insecure and wracked with pain. Upon first sight of this man using his last reserves of strength to stagger toward them, who had given so much more care than you would find in a normal person, even Oudot cried. But Terray was still rebelling against his fate and shouted in his despair and anger at the men coming toward them: "If I could only see, I would climb down alone!"

Immediately behind them came Schatz and Couzy, then Lachenal, half carried by two porters. "You should see how a mountain guide from Chamonix comes down the Himalayas!" he is reported to have said to Ichac in the camp, when he greeted him with open arms.

They had all been saved. Annapurna had been conquered and suddenly this "victory" actually meant something. Herzog, although in the worst condition, was the first to realize this. Now at last he was allowed to hand over the leadership to his friends. He would put his trust in Oudot and grow healthy again. The importance of this victory for him later on can only be understood when one knows the extent of his injuries and disabilities.

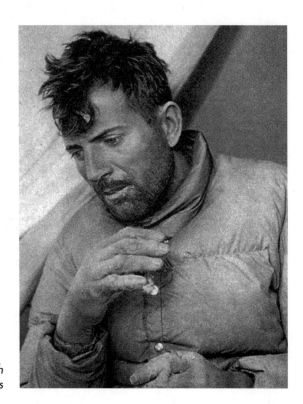

*Maurice Herzog with
frostbitten hands*

So all the members of the expedition team were in Camp II. And what a state they were in! Through the ministrations of Oudot, the doctor, all of them—with the exception of the two "summit victors"—were soon able to recover. Four of them, the rescuers, were fit again relatively quickly.

Terray and Rébuffat were soon able to go out into the sun again if supported by somebody.

Only Herzog and Lachenal were long-term patients, and the camp became a makeshift hospital. Herzog had frostbitten hands and feet, and Lachenal's toes were black. Oudot first gave both of them intravenous injections, which were very painful, and later amputations were to become necessary. When they cleared the camp, the wounded had to be carried on sledges.

Maurice Herzog was now suffering terrible pain, and Lionel Terray, who once again was playing the wild man, would become, alongside Oudot, his strongest support during his life of suffering. During the whole return trip, Terray did not merely show an almost fatherly warmth toward Herzog, it was his tender care that in the end kept Herzog alive.

It took a long time to prepare for the march back to the valley. Teams went ahead to prepare the path through the upper Miristi Khola. Lachenal was carried and the Sherpas Adjiba, Sarki, Fou-Tharkey, and Pansy had to take turns carrying Herzog in a backpack. It was a painstaking process, having

During the monsoon rains, the going gets slippery on the steep slopes of the Kali-Gandaki gorge, through which the 1950 expedition had to return after climbing the mountain.

to set him down repeatedly, the porters changing places, the many balancing acts when setting off. It was all very unpleasant for the porters and even worse for the one being carried.

Herzog: "The track is well trodden, with no more stones on it; we are marching as if on a proper path. I am squashed up against the porter. Each step is a terrible shock for me. I am afraid of falling, and cling desperately to his neck. Yet I do my best not to impede his walking. If his steps become uncertain, I sense it clearly. Sometimes Adjiba or Pansy slip. Instinctively I raise my arm to try to find a hold on a piece of rock, forgetting that my arm is useless. More than the gullies, I fear the very steep rock slabs where my porter could fall; each second I fear that my hands and feet could be knocked against the rocks."

In the torrential rain, their clothes soon became soaked. The tents, the sleeping bags—everything was soaked. The slopes and gullies were slippery; everything was dripping wet. Stones were loosening, rocks falling, as the procession went over them. This return was more like a flight after a collapse.

After days of being carried, the invalids' pressure points were so painful that Oudot gave Lachenal a morphine injection before putting him in the backpack. In the meantime a willow basket had been found for Herzog, which made the pain more bearable; he was even able to slide his legs into a sleeping bag.

With the exception of the two who had injured feet, Oudot, Terray, Couzy, Ichac, the Sherpa Sarki, and eight porters, the troop was progressing so desperately slowly along the Miristi Khola that Herzog once again gave up all hope. The porters, bent double beneath the weight of the invalids, battled on day after day; they slipped, hesitated, groaned, and then made a couple miles' (a few kilometers') progress after all. Each individual step was a problem. The evening always came too soon, and even by evening the men sat lost and imprisoned in this wet, colorless countryside. Although the porters set off again each morning without complaining, night always fell before the next camp had been reached. With the help of three torches, the three healthy sahibs often led the porters and Sherpas through the fog, the rain, and the night until at last, exhausted, fearful, and disheartened, they gave up somewhere between the black chasms, because there was no way they could carry on.

Once they built a kind of roof as a weather shelter for Lachenal and Herzog. Here they were protected and dry, and Terray stayed with them while Couzy, Ichac, and Oudot tried to reach the next camp. Late at night Sarki and Fou-Tharkey came back and brought provisions and a flask of hot coffee.

For the most part, it rained throughout the entire night. The invalids were tormented by unrest, and it was so cold that it was not only Herzog who was overcome by fear. And Lachenal's feet were by now so badly swollen that they would no longer fit into any kind of boots; Herzog's extremities began to become septic. Yet they were still too far removed from civilization for Oudot to risk amputations; the danger of infection seemed too great to him.

The Sherpas had to get the two injured men 6,500 feet (2000 m) down incredibly steep slopes into the Kali-Gandaki valley before the necessary surgical operations could be carried out.

Once, Herzog's porter was unable to move either forward or backward. He just could not move. Finally he traversed sideways off the steep slope step by step; all the while the "chair" in which Herzog was sitting hung far out over the abyss. The injured man dared not move. If the Sherpa had slipped, there would have been no rescue for either of them.

It was a miracle—how many was that by now?—that Herzog was still alive when the expedition arrived back in the Kali-Gandaki valley. Yes, they were all still alive. But Herzog still faced amputations. And it was not only the injections that grew more painful with every passing day; the sitting, the pressure of being carried, the open wounds. The team's morale had now reached its lowest ebb. Herzog said later, "The expedition now appears to have become a limp and anemic body devoid of blood, painstakingly crawling along paths, the reason for which we can no longer see. One single desire keeps us going: to reach India as fast as possible. The interminable descent, through the Nepalese valleys in the unceasing rain and the damp heat of the monsoon, is having a disastrous effect on us physically. My companions have lost their energy, they are dragging themselves miserably along the little walls of the rice fields. They walk in silence, their faces expressionless, unable to summon up interest in anything."

A column of porters on the descent: on the way home from Annapurna I

Nevertheless Herzog and Lachenal made it and the rest of the team held together. They never lost their willingness to cooperate and so, at the end, the expedition once again rose to being what it had been at the start: a small team full of youthful enthusiasm for a great and distant goal, eight men who stuck together even in times of near failure.

POSTSCRIPT

The Annapurna I group,
viewed from the north:
Tilicho, Nilgiri, Annapurna
with The Fang

VICTORY, DEATH, AND REBIRTH

If we want to look critically at the Annapurna Expedition of 1950, then we have to place the mountaineers and their actions—"I look very closely at the enemy" (Herzog)—in the context of their time and understand in whose name Maurice Herzog was acting. Certainly, on the mountain Herzog, as expedition leader, was fully responsible for logistics and team leadership, but in the period leading up to the undertaking, it was the French Alpine Club and its manager, Lucien Devies, who had pulled the strings. Yes, the sayings, which were hammered out at the head of this expedition, are the words of nationalists, of the Resistance, of colonialists. But let us first place ourselves in this postwar period in France.

After the second world war—the Resistance and the humiliation from the Germans were over—a spirit of nationalism ruled France. And all of a sudden the French were the best mountaineers in the world: active, creative, innovative. They were the design leaders in the field of new equipment—tents, sleeping bags, ice axes—and suddenly they were capable of repeating the great routes of the prewar period, the North Face of the Eiger, the Walker Spur, the Badile. Why should they not succeed where others had until now failed, with the ascents of the eight-thousanders? The mountaineers of the Annapurna team were themselves hardly even aware that in doing this they took on the rites, the oath of obedience, and in part even the language of the hated Germans, who in the period between the wars had taken their great German language as far as the Himalayas.

But be careful; it was not Herzog, but Lucien Devies who, before their departure from Paris, had demanded that they swear an oath. This oath of loyalty, which may seem merely embarrassing today, was then a prerequisite for participation in the expedition: "Now, gentlemen, I pray you take this oath as did your predecessors in 1936: 'I swear by my word of honor to obey everything that the leader of the expedition demands of me during the course of the expedition.'" Although the French alpinists too had no great love of ceremony, they all took the oath, and their inner conflict remained unspoken,

L'épopée officielle racontait un Maurice Herzog très France-qui-gagne, brandissant son drapeau. Elle occultait totalement Louis Lachenal qui était avec lui au sommet. Ses mémoires posthumes écornent le mythe.

« Ise met à courir comme un dément et crie "Il fait beau, il fait beau." Il est clair qu'il ne se rend plus compte de ce qu'il fait. » Chamonix, été 1955. Louis Lachenal est pressé. Cinq ans ont passé et ces phrases d'Annapurna, premier 8000 le hantent. Leur auteur? Maurice Herzog, le héros aux doigts coupés, le premier rôle de cette tragédie. Lachenal-le «démenti», lui, veut faire savoir à tous que c'était Herzog, l'«illuminé» et que lui, lucide, l'a arraché à l'extase

Pour mémoire
Le 3 juin 1950 à 14 heures, Louis Lachenal et Maurice Herzog au sommet de l'Annapurna (8075 m). Le soir, au camp V, ils retrouvent Lionel Terray et Gaston Rébuffat. Le 4 juin, tempête. Les quatre alpinistes se perdent et passent la nuit dans une crevasse. Le 5 juin, beau temps. Ils sont sauvés de justesse par Couzy et Schatz. Lachenal (pieds gelés) et Herzog (pieds et mains) sont amputés par le docteur Oudot.

Deux livres clés
Les Carnets du vertige. Écrits par Gérard Herzog, frère du conquérant de l'Annapurna, en 1955-1956 à partir des notes de Louis Lachenal, ils viennent d'être réédités par Michel Guérin. Deux passages sont inédits, dont les «Commentaires» de Lachenal sur l'Annapurna. Le chapitre «Journal de l'Annapurna», est rétabli

In 1996 a literary feud directed against Maurice Herzog began in France, which I found unfair. Naturally there were still unanswered questions about the report on the Annapurna ascent published in 1950, but Herzog's summit success remains an indisputable fact.

as Herzog later remembered: "My friends stood there awkwardly and at the same time moved." What else could they have done? Lucien Devies would suffer no contradiction. For him, a Himalayan expedition was like a continuation of the war: "Fight against the mountain."

Herzog said later: "For us, Annapurna was an ideal fulfilled: In our youth we would not be misled by fantastic tales or by the descriptions of the bloody fighting of modern wars, which gave food to childish fantasies. For us, the mountains were a natural fighting ground, where we could find our freedom on that boundary between life and death, which we searched for in the dark and which we need in the same way as our daily bread."

Paul Bauer, having returned from the first world war, justified his 1929 and 1931 "Kanch" expeditions in a similar way. And, as in those days, in 1950 on Annapurna, "plans for the great battle" were first drawn up, and then the risks were played down: "The dangers are relatively small." Once the troops had been "called up," it was easy to boost their "morale." After the "powwow," the "reconnaissance troops" set out, and on the express command of the Führer the "attack" could begin. "If we want to win the battle" we must "fight the great fight," Maurice Herzog wrote "in friendship" to Lucien Devies when he was already high up on the mountain.

However, after the success—to be precise, on the summit itself—the tragedy began. First there was the chaotic descent, then the fight with death. Now the heroism was well and truly gone.

In the book that Herzog later wrote, the expedition leader clearly remembers these values that had been set down at the start, values such as collective battle, collective victory, fraternity.

During the descent, all these preconceived ideas gave way to pain and fear. The comrades at the last camp did, it is true, receive "the great news" of the summit victory with "enthusiasm," but they were more aware of Herzog and Lachenal's terrible state. But Herzog himself "without knowing, still in a euphoric state," did not for one moment stop to think that he had robbed the others of their chance for the summit, and he was overcome by "an enormous sense of good fortune" when in one sentence Terray gave him absolution and justified the expedition: "As you were up on the top, it is a victory for all of us, a victory for the whole team."

Thus a "collective victory" could be salvaged from one individual's mania, and the values of the French revolution—liberty, equality, fraternity—were saved. Yes, this was precisely how the expedition had been planned: one for all, all for one, and the summit as a symbol of this. The summit victory counted as a collective ideal. And in the Annapurna book, too, this cliché had to have homage paid unto it. "This victory is not the victory of an individual, a triumph of pride—no indeed, and Terray was the first to realize this—it is a victory for us all, a victory of human fraternity."

Herzog, "imprisoned in a kind of drugged stupor," no longer heard his companion's cries for help during the descent. However, at home again, after he "had lost all contact with reality," once more he sang the song of fraternity—and this, in spite of the fact that it was his egotism that had without doubt made him go way too far on the path to the summit. The Annapurna book by Herzog and company is full of contradictions—that is what makes it so interesting.

Only when they found Lachenal—"stretched out, eyes empty, without ice ax or snowsuit, without gloves, with only one crampon remaining on his feet"—does Herzog's personal tragedy become credible. Indeed, even though Herzog—"gradually I lose consciousness"—allows us to believe even today that to die in the mountains is a beautiful thing, the facts speak against it. The sentence "I am dying in my mountains" must then be understood as the glorification of pure wishful thinking. This romanticism must surely be something that Herzog only incorporated into his writing once back home again.

We ask ourselves, "How was this near-death experience in reality?" After that awful night spent bivouacking in a snow hole, when Marcel Schatz appeared from below, there was still no transformation in Herzog: It was only later that he wrote "a wonderful apparition." It is true that once again hope was welling up within Herzog, but the situation remained one of desperate need. Schatz "fought his way forward, slowly wading up to his waist in soft powder snow." For Maurice Herzog, who needed help, certainly "a deeply distressing moment." No more than that? His eyes were glued to the rescuers coming toward him, twenty steps away, then ten. Schatz then came directly toward Herzog, and at this moment he is supposed to have come back to life. "My heart beat as he approached. Death had already stretched out his hand to me, I had surrendered. I return, life is calling me again. An enormous transformation takes place within me....No, everything is not yet lost." Thus, during the course of the book, gradually each member of the team is transformed into a lifesaver, a support for the hero, and thus a participant in the collective victory.

This Maurice Herzog, who only survived due to the obvious help from his comrades, appeared to be able to bear the exhaustion and pain and to feel able to demand sacrifices from the others, knowing that he had won success for them all. In the days, months, and weeks after the summit ascent, he went through hell, but always in the knowledge that he had done what was superhuman for them all, and therefore he had to suffer for them all. "Never have I suffered so much in my entire life," he later wrote.

Whether he would be able to keep his frostbitten hands and feet was now dependent on only Oudot and his own stamina, he thought then. That he had given his all for the summit, that he had risked everything, gave him, in his own sight, the right to remain unscathed. Herzog, a wreck and reduced to a cripple, was now not only dependent on the doctor and the help of the Sherpas and comrades, but above all on his own inner strength. He was cared for like a small child, but without the psychological crutches afforded him by his success, he would never have survived. After those days of euphoria, he was now to experience the saddest days of his life—"I have the impression that my condition is getting worse. I feel helpless and am deeply discouraged"—and at the same time he felt like a hero, like the one who had fought for everything to the bitter end and who, after reaching the target, was now suffering for everyone.

The "victory" had been his duty, and even on the back of one of these tough Sherpas, hanging over the depths of the Kali-Gandaki valley, in his fear, he was able to internalize the reason for his suffering, constantly reminding himself of his duty.

"Where is my ice ax?" he suddenly asked, and Schatz, who was walking alongside him, was shocked. Why does the patient need an ice ax? Herzog intended to give the tool of "victory" to the Club Alpin on his return, as a kind of "trophy"; after all, Lucien Devies needed a symbol for the battle for the common good. Herzog was almost submissive to this instigator to whom he owed the organization of the expedition, and thus his success, and now his suffering. But it was not only the intent to give the ice ax to Devies: "I place enormous weight upon this ice ax, as it is the only one that was on the summit of Annapurna. Lachenal has lost his and since we dismantled the final camp, no one has seen it. Schatz looks at all the Sherpas' ice axes. It cannot be found! This loss, which in itself is insignificant, sickens me deeply."

Herzog's ice ax, which they considered lost, was found again 2 days later— and his zest for life was rekindled too.

The return march turned into a catharsis for both summit men. In Lachenal, the realization that he had made mistakes grew. Herzog, on the other hand, was constantly in delirium, floating between the world of heroism and self-sacrifice and on the threshold of life and death, and not once did he think of self-criticism. Often he was indifferent to everything. His "I no longer have the strength to live" was not resignation, it was his letting himself drop into the role of sacrifice. Only in this way was he able to bear the pain and the weakness, the sideways glances of his comrades, the dirt. To be self-reproachful now would have killed him.

His lack of participation during the daily march through the paddy fields and the cries of pain as fingers and toes were amputated became everyday occurrences for the others. In addition to this, there were his nightly panic attacks in the camp: "In the middle of the night I suddenly wake up. Everything is pitch-black. A strange power forces me to sit up in my camp. Terrible fear constricts my heart, the feeling of nothingness surfaces within me, that terrible feeling of dying. Violent, deafening noises sound incessantly. Where am I? I cry out…the light is lit, and with infinite relief I realize that I am in a tent; I find myself again in my place in the expedition."

"What is it?" Ichac asks on one such occasion, and Herzog attempts to explain this terrible feeling of nothingness.

"A nightmare," Ichac reassures him. How could a living man fully appreciate the condition of a dying man? Or was it just the morphine that gave Herzog visions of death?

Only gradually, after the high-dosage penicillin injection began to take effect, did the fever subside and his condition begin to improve. The risk of a life-threatening blood poisoning was averted. The expedition leader began once again to speak, to understand what was going on around him, and soon to give orders.

Oudot continued to perform the operations on Herzog, which had by now become a matter of routine, and Herzog gritted his teeth. Once more he had begun to shoulder the responsibility, as had been his task on the summit ascent. During his descent from Camp V to the rice fields of Pokhara, he had entrusted his life to his expedition comrades.

Annapurna 1950.

What a return march!

Maurice Herzog suspected that his life plan up to this point had now come to a sudden end. He had returned from the most exciting mountain adventure in his life, knowing that he would never again be able to climb such high and difficult summits. He was overcome by melancholy during those evenings; when he sat beneath the great mountains, a great sadness emanated from everything he saw, melancholy as far as he could cast his eyes around.

Where did all this happiness, this sadness, this pain come from? "Is it the distant picture of the high valleys, the enormous mountains there on the horizon, is it the memory of that almost unimaginable use of every last ounce of strength, which we achieved in this nature? Is it the feeling that reality is becoming a dream without our noticing?" he asked himself. At the same time, however, this martyred victor began to hope and plan for a new beginning. Lucien Devies would help him achieve this. Herzog understood how to accept his rebirth as a second chance.

What a difficult challenge it must have been for Herzog, this man obsessed with mountaineering, to give his life a new direction! To know that, in the middle of his life, this way to the top had come to an end meant, first of all, the grief: "These giants of the earth stand there together, they tower up to the heavens, glimmering, a silent invocation from the gods." But for whom now? No longer for Herzog. For the "victor" who came from the heights above, they had grown to unattainable heights, farther removed with every new day. To accept the reality and to want the possible was to be the prerequisite for the second half of his life, a new life design. Thus Maurice Herzog found renewed hope, creativity, and power when he looked from the lowest point in his life up to the highest mountains in the world, which were inaccessible to him now and forever.

On the plane before the landing in France, Oudot put new bandages on Lachenal and Herzog. He wanted to make the invalids look presentable for their "reception" in their home country. "Nevertheless, when we were led down the small iron staircase, in a flash those pitiful glances from our friends ripped away the masks from our faces that we had worn until that point." No, Herzog was not to be pitied, but suddenly to have everyone crying over him as a hero changed his being. In the beginning he did not feel at all at ease in his new role, "and yet these tears in the eyes of friends, these horrified glances brought me back to reality at once."

But back to which reality? Into his second life! Suddenly, in the consciousness of others and in his own, he became the representative for all suffering victors. Due to their sympathy, his own achievement, and the sympathy of millions, Maurice Herzog had suddenly become "the hero of Annapurna."

This strange consolation that Herzog now found in his misery made him strong. Of course, he no longer needed it now in order to survive, but the others needed him and he them. Indeed, he now knew that his future had a purpose, which came above all from his newfound existence as a tragic hero.

"There are always new summits in a man's life," he maintained, and that is the motto he lived by. Annapurna had become a treasure for him, from which he could feed for a lifetime.

Annapurna 1950.
What a success!

Maurice Herzog.
What a career!
What a personality!

The exceptionally dangerous and heavily crevassed North Flank of Annapurna I. The French first-ascent route of 1950 climbed this face to reach the summit of the mountain for the first time.

View of the northern slopes of Dhaulagiri from the "French Col," which was reached by climbers for the first time in 1950

Dhaulagiri, with its 13,123-foot- (4000-m-) high South Face, viewed from the Gore Pani Pass. Far below lies the Kali-Gandaki valley.

During their attempt to find a suitable approach to the summit pyramid of Dhaulagiri in 1950, the French had this view of the Northwest Face of Annapurna I (East, Middle, and Main Summits, western shoulder, The Fang).

The hanging glacier below the southeast ridge of Dhaulagiri, which the French reconnoitered in 1950, is steep, heavily crevassed, and correspondingly dangerous.

The summit pyramid of Dhaulagiri I, viewed from the southeast. In 1950, this eight-thousander was a more difficult proposition than Annapurna I.

The Nilgiri Group, Annapurna I, and Annapurna South from the slopes of
Dhaulagiri, with the morning mists hanging late over the Kali-Gandaki valley below

There was no known access to the north side of Annapurna for the climbers on the 1950 expedition. The approach was, and remains, a complex and difficult affair, frequently plagued by bad weather and new snow.

A porter from the Kali-Gandaki valley at the rest stop at Thulo Begin

The half-mile-wide riverbed of the Kali-Gandaki lies like a strip of desert between heavily wooded slopes—the deepest valley in the world. To either side, the peaks of Annapurna and Dhaulagiri rise nearly 23,000 feet (7000 m) above the valley.

In 1950 the French Expedition—a column of porters, Sherpas, beasts of burden, and climbers—reached their starting point, Tukucha, via the Kali-Gandaki valley. Many of the valley porters walked barefoot as far as the Annapurna I Base Camp.

One of the most impressive sights in the Himalayas: the awesome cirque with the steep North Buttress, up which the French made their first attempt on the mountain in 1950

An avalanche thunders down from the Great Barrier, directly opposite the North Face of Annapurna.

The only justifiable approach to the summit wall is via the blunt rib, which splits the glacier at the foot of the mountain into two halves.

Avalanches pour down the North Face of Annapurna I almost without interruption. Because the icefalls and avalanche chutes allow precious little room for a safe route of ascent, Maurice Herzog and his team were risking a lot when he made the decision to climb quickly up this 13,000 feet (4000 m) of chaotic glacier ice and rock back in 1950.

All the possible routes on the North Face of Annapurna I are dangerous. Although the French did choose the easiest line, they still encountered great difficulties.

Nowadays four routes trace their way up the North Face of Annapurna: the Spanish Route to the East Summit (left, 1974), the Dutch Spur (middle, 1977), the French Route (below right and upper left above the Sickle Glacier, 1950), and the Northwest Pillar (right, 1995).

For the 1950 "summit victors" and their rescuers, the descent through the avalanche-prone seracs and crevasses in a storm with constant snowfall and mist was much more difficult than the ascent. It was a miracle that all members of the team managed to get out of the danger zone alive; even so, Herzog and Lachenal suffered terrible frostbite to their hands and feet.

Returning from Annapurna Base Camp, heading for the Kali-Gandaki valley

New snow in the Miristi Khola, an area frequently strafed by bad weather

Camp at the foot of the South Face of Annapurna, first climbed in 1970 by an expedition led by Chris Bonington. The route goes up the buttress on the left, taking a direct line to the little summit pyramid of the Main Summit. The Fang is visible on the extreme left of the picture.

The Himalayas: The view back
toward Annapurna, which stands on
the horizon like a wall of rock and
ice; climbed, yet not conquered

Himalayan Mountaineering 1950: The Alpinism of Conquest

For more than fifty years, the eight-thousanders remained an unattainable target. In spite of the many attempts on Mount Everest (1921–1938, 1947), on K2 (1902, 1909, 1938, 1939), on Kangchenjunga (1929, 1930, 1931), on Nanga Parbat (1895, 1932–1939), and on Hidden Peak (1934, 1936), nobody could reach the summit of any one of these highest summits on Earth. Why was this? Quite simply because in those days it was so difficult, so exhausting, and so dangerous to push forward into the Death Zone. In those days there were no fixed ascent routes, and the reconnoitering took time and energy. The equipment was primitive and heavy. For example, tents had no built-in groundsheets, hemp ropes were difficult to use and became far too heavy in wet conditions. Usually expeditions were forced to spend so much time searching for the route and carrying the equipment that the monsoon or autumn storms would arrive before those at the head of the team were anywhere near the summit. The length of time spent at high altitude meant that the climbers were exposed to the risks—avalanches, ice- and rockfall, storms, and altitude sickness—of an eight-thousander climb for far longer than the high-altitude mountaineers of today. Contemporary climbers usually only make one attempt, and climb up and down again in the shortest time possible via a chain of camps that have been set up for them; in addition, they are climbing on prepared, known, and secured routes, often with countless opportunities for turning back.

The earlier tragedies on the eight-thousanders between 1895 and 1939 repeatedly involved the most experienced mountaineers, and they were primarily responsible for endowing this prestige—unintentionally perhaps—upon the highest mountains in the world and thus making them the "third pole." Having been stylized as a myth, first by geographers and dreamers and later by journalists and returning travelers, the eight-thousanders first became a vanishing point for national pride, then an exotic destination for

Dead climber at the foot of Annapurna, found in 1985. Maurice Herzog and his men were lucky; later there were to be many fatal accidents, particularly on the French Route.

millions, and today they are a "heroes' playground," because their "challenge" has not yet been completely expended.

Right in the middle of this century of attempts and conquests on eight-thousanders lies Herzog's success and life of suffering on and as a result of his ascent of Annapurna. As if this expedition were a turning point, a kind of cutoff point between myth and banality, it makes clear just what it was that set the Himalaya apart beforehand and what it signified for mountaineering afterward.

Fifty Years Later

Every victory has many fathers, but tragedy has only one scapegoat, as it is said. Annapurna, however, was at the same time both victory and defeat, and this is what later gave rise to such discussion, argument, and judgment about the expedition and its leader, Maurice Herzog.

Even fifty years later, many mountaineers in France are clearly divided in their opinions about the "great heroes," although Herzog had from the start explained what it was all about and set the framework for the time after the expedition. His philosophy remains steadfast to the current day: common effort for the great ideal!

Even before they flew to India, Herzog had defined the great French Expedition thus: "Each of us knows that he owns nothing and that he should expect nothing upon his return." Having one clear goal was to be the force that would motivate these men to push themselves to the limits. And after the expedition, they were expected to retreat selflessly into the background. Upon their return, all personal films and diaries had to be handed over; Herzog spoke for everyone. Thus there could only ever be one Annapurna book.

Maurice Herzog has always defended the contract between the Féderation Française de la Montagne (FFM) and the participants in the expedition, and even today feels that it is completely justifiable, because "There was neither censorship nor secret that should have been jealously guarded." In his eyes, it was not necessary for several books to be published about the same adventure, because "My book was read by all members of the expedition team before its publication. Everyone was in agreement with it." Indeed, what Maurice Herzog had written was never refuted, even later on.

The fact that both Lachenal and Rébuffat had leveled criticism at the expedition leader in their expedition diaries was accepted by Maurice Herzog. Together with members of the FFM, however, it was decided to pay no further regard to this. After all, there is disappointment and dissatisfaction after every expedition. Herzog again: "You write down your feelings on paper and there they remain." His book was to be "the memoirs of the circumstances" and that is what it has remained to the present day.

Herzog found the controversy that arose from his and Lachenal's Annapurna expedition diaries to be petty. Nevertheless, he defended himself, both from a legal point of view—"the then Himalayan Committee, under the leadership of Lucien Devies, had made an exclusive deal with Arthaud for a book about our adventure"—and from a moral point of view: "There were no secrets on this expedition. Everything was said in the book *Annapurna*— the first eight thousander, and my expedition comrades, including Louis Lachenal, had approved the contents." Of course opinions were lost, critical thoughts were suppressed, and bitter reactions left out. Were they overreacting, as Herzog supposed? After all, it was the men's lives that had been at risk.

Certainly a contradictory viewpoint would have been good for the book; it would have made it seem more human. But nobody can criticize the expedition leader for what he left out.

In 1996, when Herzog was almost eighty, that nobody was prepared to come to his defense is sad—and it is only because of this that this book was written. Why was it that Maurice Herzog himself should be the one to have to point out the only conclusive argument against all this controversy? "Why was it that I had to dismantle all the camps in spite of the most terrible difficulties, and why was it that I always had to take the lead as we made our summit ascent, and in the end was the first to stand on the top?" Nobody can question the facts, and it was the facts that made Herzog right forever, and his book too. Herzog had climbed ahead of all the others this one time in his life, but the farther away he is, the smaller he becomes for those remaining behind, even for those who were later to envy him. Unfortunately.

Other Accounts

Just like Jon Krakauer's report about the Everest catastrophe of 1996, Maurice Herzog's expedition report was a more exciting read than any novel. Incredible, yet true! It is right that Herzog took all the credit for this himself—in the Annapurna summit pictures, taken by Lachenal with Herzog's camera, it was only he that could be seen with the French flag. Thus Lachenal was forced into the background. But why? Quite simply, the only summit photo of Lachenal was out of focus and the real hero, Lachenal, looked nothing like a hero! That photo was quite simply not good enough for publication or display because it was blurred—Herzog had shaken the camera. And soon Lachenal had disappeared from the interest of the public eye.

In 1951 Lachenal told Rébuffat that the Himalayan Committee had threatened to exclude him from the École Nationale de Ski et d'Alpinisme in Chamonix, his employer, if he were to publish his Annapurna story in Le Monde. And later, too, anything he attempted to publish would be vetoed, until finally in 1955 at long last Lachenal's story, his exciting life as a mountaineer, was published. Finally he was able to say what had remained unsaid about the Annapurna Expedition. And in the first instance, what he wanted was to put right the role that had been attributed to him, the part he had played in the summit ascent with Herzog. He had never been able to swallow the fact that he had been passed over and that Herzog's book portrayed him as being unclear in the head on that summit day.

He was also disturbed by the fact that in Herzog's book, he was seen as a mere "hanger-on." He was also vain; like Herzog, a human being, who deserved just as much recognition. But what disturbed him most of all was that he was represented as being "crazy" in Herzog's expedition report. How was he to defend himself? With his own version of the summit ascent, obviously. Unfortunately—and that was Herzog's great mistake—the first version was edited to suit Herzog's book. Was it this that proved to be the sticking point for Lachenal? We do not know.

Without a doubt it was Herzog who, on Annapurna, had gone way beyond his means, had risked everything, had been crazy, unable even to take a decent picture on the summit. And thus it was he who had buried Lachenal's fame. Whether Lachenal had later regretted not turning back on that morning of June 3, 1950, we do not know. One other thing continued to torment him: the situation as described by Herzog after their night in the cave. "He started to run like a madman, crying out, 'It's beautiful, it's beautiful.' It is obvious he no longer knows what he is doing" was what Maurice Herzog had written about Lachenal in this book, a book that was to be read by millions. Herzog, the hero with amputated fingers, the main character in this tragedy, had certainly not wanted to make judgments about Lachenal, but this book was read above all by people outside mountaineering, and only those who were in the know would have been able to realize that something was not quite right here.

Even if reality had been turned on its head, and Lachenal rather than Herzog had been lucid, the Annapurna Expedition would still have cost him his feet. Since June 3, 1950, he had suffered pain, operations, transplants—two years of hell. And this man Lachenal, who was no longer even much use as a mountain guide, became neither a government minister nor famous the world over.

On the other hand, however, it is thanks to Herzog's "official expedition story" that Lachenal was not completely forgotten after his death. It is true that this heroic epic places Maurice Herzog on a pedestal, but by no means does it pass over Lachenal's achievements during the summit ascent. Nor does Lachenal's memoir, which appeared posthumously in 1996, diminish Herzog's myth, because every reader who is able to transport him or herself back to 1950 will read two coinciding accounts. Of course Lachenal, too, felt the effects of the thin air at that altitude. That was normal. But was Herzog really acting like a man who had found enlightenment? No, quite the opposite: as he walked toward the summit, he had a mission to fulfill, and on the summit all he could think of was his camera. Lachenal wanted to climb down again immediately—that alone is proof enough that it was he, Lachenal, and not Herzog who had remained sane! It was only because of one man possessed that Lachenal had not turned back earlier.

During the whole ascent, Lachenal had never been concerned with France's national reputation, but with the safety of the team. That Lachenal was a mountain guide and Herzog an amateur climber counted for little. Lachenal did not want to let Herzog continue on alone, because he knew that no one would have forgiven him if he had left the expedition leader alone in the Death Zone. And because he was unable to persuade Herzog to descend with words alone, he continued climbing behind him—he could not turn back. Thus they reached the summit together. Herzog had been the driving force, Lachenal the lifesaver. One without the other would not have worked on Annapurna. To go it alone to the summit would have meant death for Herzog, and a dead "summit victor" would have been unable even to bring back the news of his heroic deed.

After Lachenal's death on November 25, 1955, it is true that Herzog looked after his widow, Adèle, as well as his two sons, Christian and Jean-Claude; his brother, Gérard Herzog, however, worked on Lachenal's first biography, which was edited and revised as a heroic song for Annapurna in such a way as to fit the frame that Lucien Devies had always wanted: one story, one hero, one message! Only in this way could the symbolic strength of Annapurna resound for all times, for all nations. Thus Lachenal did not become an antihero—as a dead man, he continued to serve the myth of a common ascent—even if he could have served as the saviour of Herzog's success. Once branded hysterical, and deemed to have been little more than a hanger-on, he could not now be allowed any kind of rehabilitation, and that was a pity.

But not only Lachenal, Gaston Rébuffat too, who had often had to grease Herzog's boots on Annapurna, no longer understood the world after he had read Herzog's book. He and Lionel Terray had welcomed them in the upper-most camp and then led them down through the storm and looked after them. How often during this time had they pacified the crazy summit vic-tors! Yet there was still more—Rébuffat and Terray had saved their lives, over and over again. Rébuffat, who had come home morally but not psychologi-cally disabled after Annapurna, intentionally stayed in the background for a lifetime, far removed from the pedestal upon which Herzog had been raised. He remained publicly silent as far as Annapurna was concerned. Was this because he, too, like all the other expedition members, had signed an exclu-sive contract, which bound him to remain silent? No. It was because he was a gentleman, a man of honor.

The Many Truths

It need not necessarily be the case that a national expedition upon which a nation places all its hopes is under more pressure to succeed than an individual attempt. Of course, the French—both at home and on the mountain—wanted this "summit victory"—as, above all, did Maurice Herzog, the expedition leader who risked too much and almost died after the summit push. His story was suitable as a heroic song, and it was easy to stylize and idealize the collective disaster of the descent as a team achievement. Thus, in the collec-tive consciousness of the public at large, Herzog and his helpers became a team, which, carried along by a wave of harmony, emerged victorious—a homogeneous team from the start to the end of the expedition.

The fact that, in Herzog's Annapurna book, the many subtle differences in the way the ascent and descent were portrayed, and the innumerable private catastrophes of this hero's story, had to be sacrificed went unnoticed by the reader. Above all the fears, which turned to aggression on the return journey, were lost in print. Thus the different truths were reduced to a com-mon ideal, as required by the spirit of the age.

But this book belonged, as did the whole "summit victory," to the plans and desires of one Lucien Devies, who had wanted the expedition to take place, had styled it with national pathos, and in the end had used it as a means of identification for the Grande Nation of Charles de Gaulle, during whose presidency Herzog was later to become a government minister.

Clearly Lucien Devies, like the German Karl Herrligkoffer after him, had copied the famous German expedition leaders of the thirties, who had failed on "Kanch" and Nanga Parbat, in order to construct his story. Because after the expedition any rights to photos and texts had to be surrendered to the FFM without any further checks, it was possible to weave his Annapurna tale and only his version. Herzog was certainly not interested in falsifying the story, but his supervisor, Lucien Devies, president of the FFM, gave the "Annapurna Heroes" a hand in order to express his very own nationalistic and moral fantasies. He presented the world with a harmonious view of expedition proceedings, the greatest possible success, a perfect conclusion with self-sacrifice, and a hero in the person of Maurice Herzog.

That Herzog did not decline to accept this role can be understood in human terms, given that after Annapurna he had no hope whatsoever of any further heroic mountaineering deeds, and the time was not yet right for a self-critical examination of his actions.

Many of the passages in Herzog's book sound as if they are fairy tales, and the characters are far too noble to be real—Terray, Lachenal, Oudot. A whole bunch of superhumans! Obviously things were very different, more human, contradictory often to the point of despair. And of course there were tensions within the team, jealousy, mistakes. This Annapurna epic, however, the tale of courage, camaraderie, loyalty after and beyond the time of the expedition, became the most successful mountaineering story of the century. This is probably also because the story corresponded to the wishful thinking of all those who could only look up to the summits, to those distant lofty ideals that are nowhere else piled up so high as in the Himalayas.

That there were tensions in the team was obvious—Herzog was capricious and not the most experienced mountaineer of all. But he was able to let Lionel Terray, whom everyone would have willingly accepted as leader, appear as a star both on the mountain and in the book. Louis Lachenal, who after all had accompanied him to the summit as a kind of mountain guide, died in a glacier crevasse before his biography was edited by Gérard Herzog.

Gaston Rébuffat, who has repeatedly told me about Annapurna from his perspective, said nothing publicly. As he grew older, he had become more and more critical toward Herzog, probably also because in the end the latter was the only figure of light to shine out of this successful yet tragic Annapurna Expedition, but he did not want to compromise him. Jean Couzy and Marcel Schatz, two mountaineers who were also extremely polite and reserved, had never expressed any criticisms toward the expedition or the book, and it was

Marcel Ichac, after all, who had delivered the facts for Herzog's great expedition report.

Fifty years after the first ascent of Annapurna, we are allowed to and must have the courage to scratch at the surface of this "heroic deed," but it would be wrong to diminish Herzog's achievements for these reasons. Once the polish has been removed from all the nationalistic and heroic phrases, we should not make the mistake of falsifying the facts merely in order to remove Herzog from his pedestal, as has been tried repeatedly in France.

During the week of the summit ascent, Maurice Herzog was physically the strongest man in the team, whether that was because he had motivated himself more highly than anyone else in the team, because he was better acclimatized than the others, or because he was possessed by the idea of "summit victory." The way in which Herzog reached the summit with Lachenal and how the pair of them made the descent to the final camp with no sense of direction is proof enough for me that they were right at the top. Their unorthodox behavior proves that they had spent a long time—too long—in the Death Zone; their frostbite shows that they had gone too far. Certainly they lacked experience at high altitudes—everyone lacked that in those days—but this fact too speaks for Herzog's success.

That in his ambition he not only risked his own life, but also that of the loyal mountain guide Lachenal, Herzog himself admits. For me this summit ascent seems like a "blindly" daring flight to the top that then resulted in a dramatic descent, during which they all became true heroes—in spite of any earlier tensions.

I do not wish to dispute the fact that there was rivalry, envy, even hypocrisy in the team as on any expedition, as Rébuffat had written in a letter to his wife. Mountaineers were and still are human beings like everyone else: they are egoistic, ambitious, and often enough blind.

Thus, after every Himalayan expedition, there are as many versions as there are participants, and each one experiences the journey from a different viewpoint. For this reason, there are only subjective truths about the Annapurna Expedition of 1950, and these are bound to contradict the "official report."

Certainly it was foolish to publish Lachenal's diaries, which were edited by Herzog's brother Gérard, after his death in a glacier crevasse in the Mer de Glace, without pointing out the omissions—particularly as the abridgements point toward the weaknesses of the 1950 expedition. But it is nevertheless still wrong to question Maurice Herzog's success, which had such terrible consequences for both himself and Lachenal. Only his "mindless" push forward into the Death Zone, about which even Herzog himself talks completely scathingly, can be criticized; it is, however, at the same time the circumstance, the trigger, and the proof for the success and tragedy of the expedition.

That Lucien Devies used Herzog and turned this "heroic deed" on Anna-purna into a national event in France, with which everyone in France could identify, is one thing; Herzog's achievement on the mountain is something else. Devies was not there on Annapurna. How far he was able to influence the manuscript of the book afterward I do not know. Devies, a master of groupings, of idealizing, reminded me, during later meetings, of those Ger-man expedition leaders of the thirties and fifties who had led their teams in the way that Devies would have liked to lead Herzog, his protégé.

All this idealizing, romanticizing, and heroizing of many mountaineers, which the Nazis had used so cleverly in order to propagate their "great" vision, were used by Lucien Devies and written on his flag as well. Thus I find it easy to understand the humanist Gaston Rébuffat, who detested all that was fascistic about the evaluation of the Annapurna Expedition, although he was much less concerned with the contrasting view of nature, as in St. Exupéry's and Nietzsche's worldviews, than with an unrealistic view of humankind.

In spite of the fact that his feet were suffering from frostbite, Lachenal accompanied Herzog right to the summit so as not to leave him alone in

that trancelike state in the Death Zone. We can assume that Herzog in his insane state—apathy in his head, tiredness in his legs, and euphoria in his heart—would have died somewhere in the summit area if Lachenal had not forced him to make the descent.

What happened afterward is proof that they had both gone too far. They had become uncoordinated, mindless, careless; they climbed, slid, and slipped down. Each man for himself. As if they no longer knew where they were or what they were doing. As if they had lost their minds! No wonder that later on they were only able to remember the details sketchily. We could ask ourselves whether they actually remembered anything at all about the events of that day. Suddenly there were two realities for them: an internal and an external. But not only for Herzog and Lachenal; many more mountaineers after them would experience this kind of schizophrenia in the Death Zone––the feeling of being both the actor and the audience at the same time, of changing sides from the (external) reality to the (inner) imagination.

Maurice Herzog was certainly not the exemplary organizer and leader that we frequently imagine an expedition leader to be. Nor was he, in

Annapurna I with the East, Middle, and Main Summits visible, together with the West Shoulder and The Fang

mountaineering terms, predestined for the summit. His strength had grown from his unconditional identification with the summit of Annapurna, the ascent as a task that he had both taken responsibility for and chosen. He showed the same stance later on during his life as a politician. Again and again, he would take on the responsibility for the families of his expedition comrades, as well as his own family and his duties in office. It is this sacrifice that makes him stand out, and for this he earns our complete respect.

Drugs and Doping

As was common practice in the fifties, the French on Annapurna took drugs, stimulants that had been tried and tested during the Second World War. The extent to which these amphetamines—Maxiton, for example—affected the soundness of mind of the summit party can no longer be measured, but the many "mistakes" during the descent can certainly be traced back to them.

In the twenties and thirties, drugs were taboo for mountaineers. Later (1950–1964), they were used repeatedly during first ascents. Only in the seventies were the risks of taking drugs, combined with the effects of high altitudes, recognized. We have now strictly rejected many kinds of stimulants. But today, when climbing eight-thousanders, there is a whole range of medication and drugs that are used: Diamox, Dexedrine, etc. In competitive sport, you would talk of doping. But mountaineering is not a sport, and back at base camp after climbing Mount Everest, nobody is going to ask you for a urine sample.

FROM THE SOUTH

The South Face of Annapurna—a couple miles wide and almost 2 miles (more than 3 km) high, it is one of the greatest of the 26,000-foot (8000-m) peak faces.

FIRST ASCENT OF THE SOUTH FACE OF ANNAPURNA 1970

Himalayan Mountaineering 1970: The Pursuit of Difficulty

Twenty years after the "conquest" of Annapurna, all fourteen of the eight-thousanders' main summits had been climbed. The mountaineers' euphoria for the great heights had died down.

The general public's interest in the Himalayas had all but blown over. The subsidiary summits, the 23,000-foot (7000-m) and 20,000-foot (6000-m) peaks, were now of interest to only a specialized audience.

When in the early 1970s a young generation of climbers dared to attempt to climb the eight-thousanders via their steepest walls, everybody was once again packing their gear and getting ready to go. The trend ushered in a new phase of mountaineering, and the highest mountains of the world

The South Face of Annapurna, showing the position of high camps 2 through 5 of the 1970 expedition. Camps 1 and 6 are hidden.

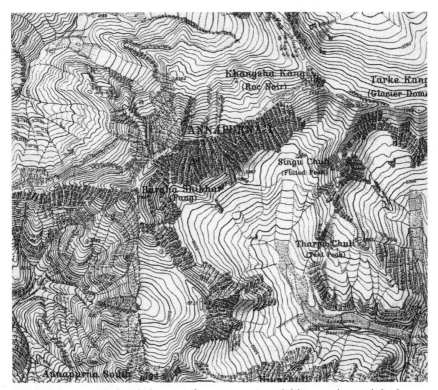

In 1970 there were detailed maps of Annapurna available, together with high-resolution photographs of the South Face and descriptions of the approach routes—a new era of 26,000-foot (8000-m) peak mountaineering could begin.

had once more become of interest to the public at large. The big faces on the eight-thousanders had suddenly begun to be seen as the final challenge in classic mountaineering. And once again it was first ascents of new routes to those summits that had captured the nations' imaginations, that would be attempted first: Annapurna, Mount Everest, and Nanga Parbat. The first ascent of the South Face of Annapurna was to become the symbol of a new era in the Himalayas.

The First Ascent of the South Face

The South Face.
The new challenge!
And a new style.

Like the French Annapurna Expedition of 1950, the South Face Expedition of 1970 was, in its own way, a unique occurrence. It was a first-class project,

*The South Face of
Annapurna I: the big
challenge in 1970*

with an outstanding leader and a host of strong personalities as expedition members, the same as twenty years before. Both expeditions—in 1950 and 1970—were to go down in mountaineering history as "the climbs of the century," defining moments in the annals of alpinism.

Only outstanding alpinists with experience gained on the great walls of the Alps and the Himalayas could set for themselves the Annapurna South Wall as a target, and once again we see what a target it was! This wall is 11,480 feet (3500 m) high, steep and extremely difficult in the middle section. Would there be a way up the face? In any case, it would take a whole new set of logistics, special equipment, and large sums of money. One was a prerequisite of the other. It was no longer the summit, which still had been climbed only once, that was important; the name of the challenge was now: "South Face."

Chris Bonington was responsible for getting together the best mountaineers in Britain for this challenge. In addition there was the excellent U.S. climber Tom Frost, who was renowned for his innovation in the field of equipment and famous in the States. Each participant recognized that this would be the chance of a mountaineering lifetime and was suitably motivated, understandably so, with such a new kind of challenge to inspire him.

An invitation was also extended to Don Whillans, who had repeatedly been Bonington's climbing partner, because of his climbing experience at altitude, although there were doubts about his undermining cynicism. In addition to this, he spent more time in the pubs than on the cliffs. He no

The holy 23,000-foot (seven-thousander) Machapuchare

longer belonged to the elite of British mountaineering, which he, together with Joe Brown, had determined for a long time in the fifties. Don Whillans! Was there anything he had not mastered? And how strong this man was! Perhaps Chris Bonington, who had become a public figure because of his photo-reporting and his mountaineering, wanted him in his team only because he was drinking too much beer back home. Whillans agreed to join the expedition, and soon after he took on responsibility for the equipment, together with Mike Thompson. Many a long month was spent planning, buying, testing, and packing.

Ian Clough, Nick Escourt, and Martin Boysen, the second cynic in the group, were invited to join the expedition because of their climbing ability both on rock and ice and because they were looking to add a new dimension to their climbing. At the time, Dougal Haston was considered throughout Europe to be undisputedly the star of classical mountaineering. Mick Burke had frequently been his partner and, like most of the others, stood by his anarchic way of life. Tom Frost, on the other hand, was a Mormon and was therefore a teetotaler and nonsmoker, and only fitted into the team because he was at the same time both creative and tolerant. Added to these star mountaineers came Mike Thompson as an organizer, Dave Lambert as doctor, and Kelvin Kent, an army officer who happened to be working in Nepal at the time, as Base Camp manager.

It was a great expedition with an advance squad, local guides, and hundreds of porters who, in spite of the snow in the great basin-shaped valley,

Mick Burke on the difficult rock band between Camps V and VI

wound their arduous way up between Annapurna I and Machapuchare. The first three camps were quickly set up because the path through the lower icefalls and up an almost 3,300-foot- (1000-m-) high snow gully had been mapped out by nature in advance and was not hard to find.

After the third camp, the steep wall itself began. The air became thinner, the climbing more difficult. The most difficult part was to find a line. Alternating leads and climbing as ropes of two, the Britons and the Americans took turns to gain height. Whoever had completed his task would return to Base Camp in order to recuperate. It was said to have been the most comfortable Base Camp from which any eight-thousander ascent had been undertaken.

After Don Whillans and Dougal Haston had set up the route to the fourth camp—it had been necessary to make a detour to the left in order to avoid the ice storms on the ridge—Nick Escourt and Martin Boysen pitched a heavy "Whillans Box," the most stormproof tent available at the time, on a flat snow incline beneath a corniced ridge, and spent their first night at this Camp IV. "Don't be held back by the ice storms," Don Whillans had joked before he climbed down to Base Camp with Haston. Full of expectations and nevertheless troubled by doubts in this lonely place, Escourt and Boysen waited for the morning.

The ice storms between Camps IV and V made it a hard slog for them. This stretch was reconnoitered section by section, climbed, and secured with fixed ropes. Often it took the men three hours for just one rope length, and they were frequently forced to make pendulum traverses. It was rare that the

Ian Clough carrying loads between Camps IV and V

lead team actually made it as far as they had planned to in the morning or as far as the others had expected.

Ian Clough and Chris Bonington continued where Boysen and Escourt had left off; the latter had completely worn themselves out. Yet the route to the top grew more and more dangerous and, in addition, it was hidden from view. Vertical rock steps had to be climbed, and detours made around overhanging ice sections, so that the advance rope often gained only about 16 feet (5 m) per hour, and sometimes less than 100 feet (30 m) per day; and all that on a 11,500-foot- (3500 m-) high steep wall. The summit was still more than 3,300 feet (1000 m) above them.

By now it was the end of April, so there was barely a month left before the start of the monsoon. There was no room for experiments.

Once Boysen and Escourt were back at Base Camp and resting, Whillans and Haston set off again in order to relieve Clough and the expedition leader. In fact Bonington managed, with different partners and finally together with Dougal Haston, to overcome the most difficult section of the route and to reach easier territory, but in doing this he had completely drained himself and would never completely recover during this expedition.

Although there may have been so many differences between the Annapurna expeditions of 1950 and 1970—the French were less choosy about their route; the higher they climbed the more chaotic their actions became; they lacked coordination; the British, on the other hand, were following a relatively safe route and had a very cleverly devised strategy—in one way the

Dougal Haston

expeditions were remarkably similar: in the actions of their leaders on the mountain. Herzog and Bonington frequently climbed ahead of their teams, above all when their expeditions ground to a halt and threatened to fail. In this way not only were important feet (meters) gained, but potential conflict dissipated and team spirit strengthened.

Nevertheless, jealousy and criticism were not entirely absent from Bonington's team. In 1970 when half the estimated time had already been used, Bonington was exhausted, and the route was still far from climbed, nervousness reared its ugly head. Some wanted to push ahead up the face at a faster pace, many wanted to climb to the top, and, of course, all of them wanted, finally, to stand on the summit.

At the same time, it was extremely important to carry heavy loads, a task that on vertical passages and traverses was both difficult and exhausting, and could not be accomplished by any of the Sherpas. Provisions had to be taken to the top camp on an almost daily basis, and the route to the uppermost camp grew longer and longer. The team in the lead needed ropes, tents, and pitons if it was to carry on establishing the route to the top. The pyramids of the load bearers therefore grew higher, the summit aspirants grew fewer, and thus the logistics more and more difficult. Mick Burke and Tom Frost, for example, carried loads for as long as it took to set up Camp V, then they too were completely exhausted.

Again it was Haston and Whillans who would have to extend the fifth camp. After a provisional interim camp, they climbed, in spite of the bad weather, up to beneath the rock barrier, which sealed off the upper third of the wall. They pitched a tent between a few crevasses and vertical snow at the foot of the rock wall. They searched for a way around the vertical pillar, and saw hardly any opportunities. There was just one possibility remaining:

up the left side. Haston—skilled, light, and eager to explore—was almost always in the lead, and the experienced Whillans directed him from below. "Like a master with his dog on a lead," he joked.

When the two of them had climbed back down to Base Camp again, Tom Frost and Mick Burke took over the work of pushing the route at the head of the expedition. First they climbed straight up from Camp V, then they crossed over to the left into a giant dihedral in order to tackle the crux sections of the route on the way to the summit. If only they could make it as far as Camp VI!

As difficult as the terrain was—ice fields, steep rock steps, gullies—down below at Base Camp, where the progress of the lead rope was being observed through binoculars, everyone was optimistic and eager to get going. On the next team changeover, it had to be possible to reach the summit. They all now wanted to push ahead, right up to the top. Haston and Whillans set off again too, hoping that this would be for the last time. The lower camps were merely used as stations for passing through; they were mainly empty, with equipment and teams concentrated between Camp III and Camp V.

Chris Bonington, who had overdone it and was sick from carrying all the heavy loads, was the first to turn back. He had to reach Base Camp. Because time appeared to be in short supply, he had suggested that Haston and Whillans, being the fastest rope, should go for the top. Mick Burke, however, was not only tired, he was also aware that it was more demanding to take over the carrying of loads than to go ahead and fix ropes. Arguments broke out. It was less a matter of rivalry between the teams—all of them were

Annapurna I from the south. The Bonington Route climbs the left-hand of the three prominent pillars to the Main Summit.

too strong in character to allow themselves to take on the role of mere facilitator—and more a case of frustration at the slow progress, which first triggered feelings of helplessness and then aggression.

Haston did not say anything; he hardly ever said anything. Whillans, however, who had worked himself up to top form, and who as deputy leader was in a position to do so, gave the orders. He wanted to put himself and Haston on the top. This was definitely the right decision, no matter how annoyed Frost, Escourt, Boysen, and Burke were about it. Such a great expedition on such a difficult wall could only be successful if the fastest rope took over the lead.

Nick Escourt and Martin Boysen would have liked to go to the top after Mick Burke and Tom Frost had wrested the line from the wall section by section. In the meantime, they all knew that it was much harder work to transport the loads between Camps IV and V than to climb ahead. Why couldn't Whillans and Haston take care of ferrying the supplies? They were all capable of climbing ahead and fixing the ropes; only the strongest could carry the loads.

After Frost and Burke reached the end of the extreme difficulties and thus the site for Camp VI, at least they were able to climb down to Base Camp with the satisfaction of knowing that that they had found the key to success. The fixing of the rock band had been their achievement!

One has to think back thirty years in order to credit the achievement on Annapurna with the recognition it deserves. Think how heavy the equipment was, the tents, the ropes, and how primitive the technical equipment, ice axes, crampons, pitons. And none of the high-altitude porters had dared to climb above Camp III. Bonington's men had to do everything for themselves, cooking, climbing, taking their share of the lead. There was none of the comfort of the modern-day commercial expeditions. Only what the team did for itself got done. Just like the French on the north side in 1950, the British in 1970 only made progress on the South Face because the best mountaineers of their time were working together, pooling their energies. In spite of the jealousy, in spite of the anger and, at times, in spite of hopelessness.

The Annapurna South Face Expedition was the first great modern expedition to be managed like an industrial undertaking. Their leader did not direct his people from below; he was on hand, ready to jump in whenever any weaknesses surfaced.

Although he was still ill, Bonington now returned to the high camp in order to carry out support work for the lead team. The Whillans/Haston rope took over the lead as he had wished. Not only Tom Frost and Mick Burke, who had been on the wall for four weeks, seemed exhausted, but Martin Boysen and Nick Escourt were also tired, drawn from carrying the heavy loads. The four of them had worked together brilliantly and no longer had the strength to establish Camp VI quickly before the monsoon arrived, or to make their own bid for the summit, however much they would have liked to.

They made space for Whillans and Haston. Although they must have found it hard to agree to this, they knew that this was the only team who would have any chance of reaching the summit. And only because they had gotten so high were Whillans and Haston able to muster renewed hope.

When Boysen and the new summit team attempted to reach Camp VI after a bad night in Camp V, Martin Boysen, exhausted from the long time he had been working at high altitude, had to give up; frostbite and exhaustion forced him back down. What happened next was risk management at the highest levels of perfection. Time was pressing due to the imminent approach of the monsoon, and the conditions required for a summit bid had not yet been achieved.

It took Haston and Whillans a whole day to make a platform for Camp VI in the ice with their ice axes, a full day's hard labor at 24,600 feet (7500 m). Then Dougal Haston's rucksack, together with his sleeping bag and personal equipment, slid down the mountain away from his grasp. So he climbed down to Camp V, spent the night there, and rejoined Whillans at Camp VI the following day.

Amid constant snow slides, the pair fixed further rope railings in a gully starting on the left of Camp VI and leading up to a pillar on the rock band beneath the summit. At the end of the third day, and before they had reached the end of the gully, they ran out of rope, thus continuing to climb without ropes, and soon made it to easier terrain.

Later on they were able to make it back to Camp VI with no further problems. The following day, while attempting to carry a tent up, they walked straight into a snowstorm, which soon became a life-threatening situation. It was only with great difficulty that they were able to make it back to the fixed ropes, rappel down, and reach Camp VI. Luckily for them, Bonington and Clough were already there with equipment and provisions.

Since it was too late for the pair to climb down, the four of them forced themselves into the tiny tent. They spent the night in close confinement, worrying and unable to sleep properly. Outside the storm raged. It was hell.

The bad weather lasted for days; activity on the face almost died out. New snow and fog made their existence even harsher. Only Bonington was still in a fit state to carry loads from Camp V to Camp VI; they were only lightweight rucksacks, but they maintained the connecting thread to the summit team and thus kept the hopes of victory alive.

In the same way that Herzog, expedition leader in 1950, forced his expedition onward, in 1970 Bonington worked harder than anyone to save his expedition from failure. The sick expedition leader, who was providing for Whillans and Haston in Camp VI so that the pair would be able to avail themselves of any last chance should it arise, stood as a symbol for the solidarity of the group in 1970.

On May 27 they were ready for the summit push. Whillans began to climb using the fixed ropes. It was 7:00 A.M. Haston followed 10 minutes later. It was cold, colder than anything the two of them had ever experienced in the mountains before. They abandoned the plan to establish a Camp VII at about midday. After leaving behind everything that they did not absolutely need, they set off to make their way straight to the summit. With no load, and relying on their instincts, the pair now made rapid progress, Whillans always in the lead. A ledge that breaks through the short summit ridge diagonally upward from right to left, as if carved by a giant hand, provided them with the the ideal line of ascent. The two men looked at one another through ribbons of fog when they rested. After realizing that the last steep step, a mixture of rock and snow, seemed to be possible, they even managed to feel something approaching amazement.

Suddenly Whillans saw the flat snow ridge above him and, ramming the shaft of his ice ax into the névé, pulled himself up on it one final time and stood on the summit of Annapurna I. While on the south side it had been growing more and more stormy and snowing more and more heavily since

The first of the monsoon mists on Annapurna. Ian Clough lost his life in an avalanche in the icefall on the left.

midday, the weather on the north side was beautiful. There was no wind either. How flat the terrain was there!

When Haston, who had been carrying the film camera and rope, reached the ridge, Whillans hammered a piton into a large rock boulder, threaded the rope through the eyelet, and threw it south into the abyss. Then the two British men, one filming the other taking photographs, climbed leftward across the névé dome to the highest point. The third attempt on Annapurna, and the first via the South Face, had been successful.

In the space of a few days, two British ropes had reached this summit, one from the north, one from the south. After a complete break of twenty years, a new era had dawned for the "Goddess of the Earth," as the locals had named Annapurna, and for all the other eight-thousanders.

As Don Whillans looked around and saw the surrounding summits popping up and then disappearing back into the clouds, he probably suspected that climbing the South Face of Annapurna had been the pinnacle of his climbing career. What a success it was! But Dougal Haston had only just entered into this kingdom, which suited his character better than the granite towers of Patagonia or the North Face of the Eiger. Until his untimely death in 1977, he would remain an amazingly gifted high-altitude mountaineer. It is precisely the image of his character, revealed during this first ascent of the South Face of Annapurna, coolly critical, safe, and motivated, that has endured in our memories.

The second aspirant summit team comprised Mick Burke and Tom Frost. Their attempt failed. Then on May 30, when the expedition was almost over and everyone was on the way back to Base Camp, a few Sherpas, Ian Clough, and Mike Thompson were caught in an ice avalanche between Camp II and Camp I. Clough was unable to escape it and died beneath a giant ice boulder.

In spite of the great success, which rested upon joint effort and a little bit of luck too, after this fatal accident, the team sank into grief and helplessness. A single fall, at a moment when nobody was thinking of the dangers anymore, meant the death of a friend.

The shock still clung to the expedition long after the men were back home again. As if they had pushed forward into a kingdom on the far side of the human world from which you either do not return at all or you return changed, they now slowly found their way back to their daily routines. It was almost as if they had been temporarily unaware of the fact that high-altitude climbing is and always will be dangerous.

So for a third time a young generation of mountaineers had to learn that happiness and grief grow with the size of the mountain. Danger and high altitude go hand in hand and cannot be separated. The pioneers had extolled the eight-thousanders and at the same time warned us about them. They were right.

POSTSCRIPT

The summit ridge of Annapurna I, viewed from the east. Storm-force northern winds are blowing plumes of snow over the South Face.

THE ANNAPURNA TRAVERSE 1984

At the International Sports Trade Show in Munich in the early eighties, I was approached by a young Swiss man. He wanted to go to the Himalayas; no more, no less. His name was Erhard Loretan and he was a carpenter by profession. I had never heard or read his name anywhere, but I immediately saw the great dreams that possessed this gaunt young man.

Fifteen years later, this same Erhard Loretan is known as the most significant high-altitude mountaineer of his generation, but has faded forever into the background, vanishing from the scene in the same way that he appeared. Nowadays he is again pursuing his trade as a carpenter and hardly concerns himself at all with the mountaineering scene. What I find most interesting about this character is not the fact that he has climbed all fourteen eight-thousanders—it is the way he did it that is remarkable. And what inner spiritual power this man Erhard Loretan has—the traverse of Annapurna, which he accomplished with Norbert Joos, is an example of this.

Erhard Loretan could not come to terms with the limits that his existence imposed upon him and as a result he became the innovator in the game of 8000-meter mountaineering. Do we need any further explanations? No; the

On a knife edge: Swiss climbers Erhard Loretan and Norbert Joos followed the narrow crest of the ridge between the South Face and the north flank, finally reaching the summit after several days.

questions asked by nonclimbers rendered him speechless, and even most of the specialists had little idea of what he was up to. So he remained silent.

"The public does not understand why we climb 8000-meter peaks, and it does not tolerate the refusal to provide an answer. But how can you explain what goes on up there to people who have never even climbed the smallest hill?" he once defended himself during a heated TV debate. Erhard Loretan was, and still is, "under the spell of the mountains." The title of his book says as much.

We ought not to portray Erhard Loretan as a victim of the absurd, however. He was, just like Lionel Terray, a "conquistador of the useless," but he went about his business with both sense and sensibility. For me, he is the prototype of the independent mountaineer. And only such a man could have survived the traverse of Annapurna; lesser mortals would have been driven mad even attempting it.

In the post-monsoon period of 1984, he approached Annapurna I from the east, together with a Swiss Expedition. Several climbers were involved in establishing the camps as far as Camp III, situated at a height of 22,738 feet (6900 m). On October 21, as soon as the access to the East Ridge had been made safe, the "crazy trip" Loretan had at first only dreamed about could finally begin.

The weather was fine, but too warm. High up on the ridges, plumes of snow could be seen. Starting out from Base Camp, Joos and Loretan reached Camp II at about midday. It was only the following morning that Loretan explained his secret plan to his partner, Norbert Joos: to traverse the two subsidiary peaks, climb the Main Summit, and then descend to the north, down into uncertain territory.

The great southeast-to-northwest traverse of the mountain began in the glacial basin to the right of the South Face of Annapurna, seen here behind the author.

The Swiss pair climbing up to the Roc Noir from the south

"To make up the lost days, we ought to go straight up to Camp IV," Loretan reckoned. Joos was surprised, but agreed to the plan. At about six o'clock they set off. Highly motivated, yet at the same time fearful of the magnitude of the task they had set themselves, they climbed as fast as they could. From here on they climbed as a rope of three: Erhard Loretan, Norbert Joos—and Fear. By 1:30 in the afternoon, they were standing on the top of the Roc Noir, at an altitude of 24,573 feet (7485 m).

The "big ride" now began—four days between Heaven and Earth—right along the crest of Annapurna's East Ridge, which is 4.4 miles (7 km) long and continuously exposed. They spent their first bivouac in a snow cave, and on October 23 they set off, carrying all their equipment to enable them to do the complete traverse of the big ridge in one push, without having to make repeated forays from any camps.

The wind had eased, and at 5:30 A.M. they were ready for takeoff; it was time to head for the East Summit. Soon they had to negotiate an extremely exposed rock wall; Loretan belayed Joos as he climbed the steep slabs, then he seconded the pitch, and at only 8:30 A.M. they reached the col at the base of the East Summit. Only 1,600 feet (500 m) of vertical height remained, and the first stage of the climb would be done. The snow was hard, there was no need to break trail, and so they climbed quickly, each of them finding his own rhythm.

After 9 hours of climbing, they finally reached the East Summit. A cold wind, blowing hard as is always the case at this altitude, blew the spindrift into their faces.

Without hesitating—it was as if the question of whether to continue simply did not cross their minds—they descended to the col that lies between

A view from the south of the whole length of the East Ridge of Annapurna

the East and Middle Summits. Would their reserves of stamina and their strength be enough to last the course? To be sure, they were programmed to climb the Main Summit, but how far away was it still? The descent to the col was not difficult, but the wind snatched at their big rucksacks and evening soon came. Down at the col, they had had enough for the time being. They radioed Base Camp and announced to their companions their intention to go for the Middle and Main Summits as well and to descend via the North Face.

They dug a hole in the drifted snow in which to spend the night, melted snow for drinks, and, at about 26,250 feet (8000 m), settled down to wait for morning. The wind was blowing from the northwest. It was a terrible night. How was it that they could stand it up there, their bodies racked by shivers from the biting cold? How could they peel themselves out of their snow-plastered sleeping bags the following morning? Why was it that they forced cold feet into boots stiff with ice and carried on climbing, heading for the summit? No one knows the exact answer, not even the two men themselves.

At about ten o'clock they were on the Middle Summit and started down to the col below the Main Summit. Suddenly, however, they found themselves standing on the edge of an unclimbable 330-foot (100-m) precipice. They had only two pitons with them, two incalculably precious rock pegs. Should they sacrifice them now? They rappelled off the pitons, deposited their rucksacks at the notch, and climbed up the last section of the ridge to the Main Summit of Annapurna.

An hour later they were standing on the tenth-highest summit on Earth. It was 1:30 P.M. on October 24, 1984.

The feeling of elation at having made the first ascent of the East Ridge of Annapurna, with its three summits (East, Middle, and Main) was dampened slightly by the attendant worry that they might not actually be able to do the first complete traverse of a Nepalese eight-thousander, for they first had to get themselves back down the North Face of Annapurna in one piece! Because retreat back down the East Ridge was out of the question—the unclimbable band of cliffs effectively cut off their retreat—they were now obliged to embark on a true adventure, a descent into the unknown.

Carefully, they first climbed down snow slopes; each step could have been their last. For 2½ days it went on as, again and again, the abyss opened up anew beneath them.

Their sole aid to orientation on this huge North Face was a postcard they carried with them, as they attempted to weave a way between the tottering seracs and vertical rock bands, "steering a passage through that narrow zone that separates life from death," as Loretan later defined his thoughts on survival in the mountains. Lower down, Loretan and Joos decided to opt for the Dutch Route. But how were they supposed to find it?

At an altitude of about 22,300 feet (6800 m), they set up their third bivouac. While sorting out their gear, they lost a tent pole, which went sliding down the face to end up 330 feet (100 m) below on an inaccessible ledge. Pitching the now slack tent, they then made tea and thin soup so they would at least have something to drink. The fabric of the tent flapped in the violent wind, while below them an icefall gaped. Their entire collection of climbing gear now consisted of only two pairs of crampons, two axes, a 165-foot (50-m) length of 5mm rope, and a single, solitary ice screw.

It was now October 25; the sun would soon be up, but they could not wait that long and so, at about 8:30 A.M., they resumed their descent, heading first for the upper part of the Dutch Route, a spur that might mean either salvation or death for them. The ice was in poor condition and there were seracs everywhere. Three hundred feet (100 m) below was a fixed rope, a sign that this place had not always been devoid of human presence. The two Swiss—in a horrifically exposed position between vertical walls of ice—felt like prisoners trapped in a vertical world. What could they do? Move across onto the French Route perhaps? In their exhausted condition, this was impossible. They would have had to climb back up too far. So, although well aware of the risks, they continued down, Joos in the lead and Loretan following behind him. There was no other way out.

By a series of audacious rope maneuvers, bordering on desperation, they gradually lost height and finally arrived at an area of steep, smooth ice. Finding themselves in a life-threatening situation again, they decided to unrope, because if one of them was to slip and fall, it was better that he should fall alone. This was not a selfish attitude, but a selfless gesture by both men—if they had stayed roped up, one of them could have dragged the other off with him.

Once the vertical seracs on the North Face of Annapurna were above Joos and Loretan, the descent became easier, but more dangerous, for them.

In this manner, they climbed down the 65-degree ice slopes, each responsible for himself, on the front points of their crampons and with only one ax apiece, finally coming across some old fixed ropes that they were able to follow for a while.

At about four o'clock in the afternoon, they were on the big plateau at the foot of the steep northern slopes, the run-out area for all the avalanches that pour down Annapurna. Among the old debris of a previous expedition's camp, they came across the body of a Sherpa, but they could find nothing to eat among the rubbish. They spent that night out in the open, wrapped in their sleeping bags, huddled beside a boulder. They quenched their thirst from a puddle of water and even managed to sleep intermittently.

On the morning after, they were first shocked awake by the thunder of an avalanche, but the second shock was in their cold-blooded reaction— they simply pulled their sleeping bags over their heads and hoped for a last little piece of good luck, keeping tight hold of their ice axes and waiting it out, not even daring to take a look. The pressure wave hit first, then the avalanche. But they survived. Badly shaken and fueled by the fear and shock that remained within their subconsciouses after so many threats, they ran for the moraines at the edge of the glacier. Back on firm ground, and with a new future before them, they reached the Base Camp of a Japanese/Czechoslovakian Expedition a little while later, two starving ghosts of men.

And then they began to resume their normal lives.

MY ROUTE

The 9,800-foot-(3000-m-) plus Northwest Face of Annapurna, first climbed in 1985 via the concave depression to the right of the fall line from the summit

ANNAPURNA NORTHWEST FACE 1985

Himalayan Mountaineering 1985: The Minimalist Approach

Within a fifteen-year period, many of the steepest and biggest faces on the eight-thousanders were climbed: the Rupal Face of Nanga Parbat, the Southwest Buttress and South Face of Makalu, the North Face of Kangchenjunga, the Southwest Face of Everest, and the South Face of Cho Oyo. Only the extremely difficult walls like the South Face of Lhotse and the West Face of Makalu still held out despite repeated attempts, and were considered "impossible." Yet it could only be a question of time before these last bastions of rock and ice were to fall as well.

The Northwest Face of Annapurna, viewed from an airplane. The Messner Route takes a line between the two prominent rock pillars (North Pillar of Annapurna I, North Pillar of Sans Nom).

Climbing techniques, above all on ice, had undergone revolutionary improvements, and the modern equipment, made of Kevlar™, titanium, and Gore-Tex, was very good and very light. Footwear too had developed; it was now lighter yet still managed to deliver improved insulation. Back in the early 1970s, every other "8000 summiteer" had suffered frostbitten feet on his ascent, but with the advent of multilayered plastic boots, even a bivouac in the Death Zone became bearable.

From the mid-1970s onward, a new style became widespread. The small, self-contained expedition—without high-altitude porters, without oxygen apparatus, and without an attendant army of helpers—started to create a furor. Solo ascents and *integrale* traverses of the big eight-thousanders became possible. For a brief period, the "conquest" of the Big Walls lost its appeal, and Alpine style seemed to establish itself as the norm. A little later however, the "Normal Routes" saw overlapping expeditions from all over the world competing for space, and these "dinosaurs" with their hundreds of helpers stomping along preprepared tracks suffocated the creativity of an entire generation of young climbers.

Back in 1950 Maurice Herzog, as the boss of his expedition, was the "court of last appeal"; his was the final word, which everyone had to obey. The team had even sworn a written oath of obedience, and the boss considered that it was his place to lead his troops from the front. The fact that, in the end, it was Louis Lachenal who went with him to the summit even though he was not prepared to sacrifice his toes—and even less his life—for "the honor of France" certainly had nothing at all to do with obedience. It was a matter of responsibility, the feeling of responsibility of a climber who knew that Herzog would perish if he left him alone up there, that induced him to follow his boss to the top. For Lachenal, who felt ill at ease in the Annapurna team, mountaineering was a purely personal matter and in Herzog he saw neither a good organizer nor a skilled team leader. In spite of these reservations, he still followed his unloved boss to the summit of the mountain. Although he wanted to descend, because it was clear to him that they should turn back, he finally followed on behind Herzog who, throwing caution to the winds, simply pressed on through the storm and the cold.

Lachenal felt responsible for Herzog—after all, they had set off on the climb together and he, Lachenal, was without doubt the better climber. For him, it was neither a matter of national prestige nor any thoughts of climbing the first eight-thousander and the attendant fame this would bring. For Lachenal, what counted most were values such as the integrity of the climbing partnership, responsibility, safety, and the welfare of his companions.

In 1970, on the South Face Expedition led by Chris Bonington, the approach to a difficult new route on a 26,000-foot (8000-m) peak was different from that of the "conquest phase" between 1950 and 1964. Bonington had a totally different view of his role as leader, different even from the model adopted by his predecesor Herzog. Bonington frequently climbed at the head of his team, and he carried heavy loads up to the high camps, but he let other climbers make the final summit push. He represented the team publicly, during the preparation phase at home in England, on the mountain, and afterward. He assumed the responsibility for the safety of the team, equipment procurement, and the financing of the expedition. And, together with his people, he was constantly engaged in developing and redeveloping the strategies and logistics necessary for the climb. The death of his friend Ian Clough hit him harder than it at first appeared; he lived with this responsibility.

The First Ascent of the Northwest Face

When I set off for Annapurna in 1985, I had a permit, a budget, and a small, young team. But I had no tactics. It was only at Base Camp that we were to make any decisions—collective decisions—about how we were to going to tackle the Northwest Face. Although on paper, and in discussions with the officials in Nepal, I was designated as the leader of the expedition, once on the mountain I saw myself merely as the one who was there to voice the collective decisions that we made. The image of the leader had changed in mountaineering too, from the giver of orders to the integrator and, finally, to the "ideator."

Reinhold Messner in 1985 on the Northwest Face of Annapurna

On this expedition, I saw my job primarily as leading a small group of relatively inexperienced high-altitude mountaineers in to Base Camp and advising them during the preparations for their summit bid. Naturally, I also wished to get to the top of the mountain myself, but not necessarily as a member of the first team.

A year earlier, in April 1984, I had studied the Northwest Face from the opposite slopes with Friedl Mutschlechner and had come to the conclusion that it was doable. My friend Mutschlechner refused to participate in the project, however. "Too dangerous," he argued.

This face, the Northwest Face, seemed to Mutschlechner to be too steep and too exposed to the danger of rockfall; furthermore, it was a trap for bad weather. It was questionable whether it could be climbed at all, and as for the descent? Were the odds too unfavorable to justify an attempt? And was it even thinkable that a descent might be made back down the same face? To be sure, it was more problematic than the ascent and very risky, particularly after a fresh fall of snow. The face is concave, and all the avalanches meet up in the middle section of my proposed route, which meant that if the weather suddenly took a turn for the worse, the wall could become a mantrap.

The strongest man in the team was Hans Kammerlander. There had never been the slightest doubt that he would come on the Annapurna trip, it went without saying, but when he stood below that face—a man who could judge the steepness and the objective dangers of such a line immediately—even he

Reinhard Patscheider, a very fit mountaineer from South Tyrol, missed his chance on Annapurna. He died in a mountaineering accident in 1998.

was gripped by fear. "Annapurna is a mountain that always poses a threat: constant rockfall, constant avalanches, constant wind," he was to say after a reconnaissance foray to the foot of the face, so we made the decision to take a look at the North Face too, just to be on the safe side.

The route climbed by the first ascent party interested us not only because of its history—by which route exactly had Louis Lachenal and Maurice Herzog climbed the first of the fourteen eight-thousanders back in 1950?—it was also of interest to us as a possible backdoor, an escape route from the summit back down to the valley. Should our attempt to climb the dangerous and extremely difficult Northwest Face fail, we might be able to bail out onto the French Route, or even use it as a means of descent if, after climbing the Northwest Face, we found it was impossible to down-climb our route.

New routes on the big mountains had always been a priority with me. As long as I was still strong enough, I always went for the first ascents. To visualize a new route, to plan the corresponding expedition, to develop the logistics for the ascent, and then to put the whole thing into practice with a small group of friends up there in the mountains was like creating my own little world. I felt like an artist; dream and reality would merge into one.

The idea always came first; I would think of a climb, a goal would emerge, and with a little luck I would be able to realize the idea, to experience the dream as reality. This gave me the feeling of being at one with my daydreams. Never did I experience such self-knowledge as in the moments after a first ascent that I had accomplished exactly in accordance with my preconceived

Reinhard Schiestl, a sensitive man and an excellent climber from North Tyrol, was predestined for a summit push; unfortunately, he was unsuccessful.

ideas. Often I felt like an architect or a painter, and the line I had climbed gave me a feeling of pride.

All of my routes, therefore, began with a creative act and when it was all over, I did not feel the necessity to defend or justify my actions, even for a single moment. The routes climbed, and those climbed in my mind's eye, my routes, were proof enough for me of the meaningfulness of my actions. I was less interested in their perceived usefulness.

Unfortunately, I was unable to realize all my ideas. Often the necessary expeditions were just too costly or too risky. But I learned to live with this, in the same way as I learned to live with failure.

In those days, although I was forty years old, I still tried to put "impossible" ideas into practice, even those with a risk of failure. As I grew older, however, I would more and more frequently look around for alternative solutions once on the mountain, to avoid taking too many risks. I would only sidestep the issue and go for the "Normal Route" when absolutely convinced that there could be no hope at all of finding a solution to the problem I had originally envisaged.

Hans Kammerlander was also ambitious enough in those days to seek out the new and difficult routes and not to follow the well-trodden paths of the consumerist mountaineers. "The ascent of an eight-thousander by a route that has been preprepared by others would not completely satisfy me," he said, and he viewed our reconnaissance march to Nilgiri Peak more an acclimatization jaunt than a search for alternative solutions.

Hans Kammerlander, the strongest man in Messner's 1985 Annapurna team

Memorial at the foot of Annapurna I

There was nobody at the French Base Camp, but we did find the names of many of our predecessors who had died on Annapurna chiseled into some rocks—the list read like a warning.

"A dangerous mountain," said Hans.

"Maybe we will be lucky," I said.

"You have to be prepared for luck."

"And for the dangers."

We continued on toward the mountain.

"Our face has been tried plenty of times," I said during a short rest break. "Yes, but left and right of our line," Hans interrupted our climbing a short while later.

"But they were all unsuccessful."

"And why did they fail?"

"Because they all avoided the logical route."

"Avalanche threat. I am worried about that too."

"Me too."

"There are avalanches everywhere around here."

"We will just have to take care not to get caught under their wheels," Hans said, and we stamped farther uphill.

Again there was this huge plume of snow hanging from the summit of Annapurna; the mountain looked like a gigantic locomotive.

If we were to make my idea reality, we would have to use every available opportunity, and this meant we had to be ready to move at a moment's notice. Remaining flexible enough to deal with the unexpected is often half

Climber to the left of the first belt of seracs in the middle part of the Northwest Face of Annapurna

the battle. Maybe a long period of fine weather would arrive, maybe this would coincide with our reaching our best form, maybe the snow conditions would be good for only a week. Choosing the right moment was just as crucial as having the right partner. It was worth waiting for such moments.

Meanwhile, the mists had descended.

We were climbing up the edge of a moraine when Hans suddenly quickened his pace. Was that not a mummified hand sticking up out of the snow? Yes, there was a body lying there! But this bony hand did not make me feel sad. In the swirling mists, it looked like a sculpture. The fingers were dessicated and black. With the gray of the snow all around, the skeletal hand looked ghoulish. The body too, which lay beneath a thin covering of new snow, reminded me more of a mummy from a bygone age than a dead climber. A strange feeling of distance overcame us, as if we had nothing at all to do with the dead man.

This image, seen through the first flakes of a fresh fall of snow as we walked past on our way to the foot of Annapurna, had nothing horrifying about it. It was as if death belonged here in this bizarre glacial world, and

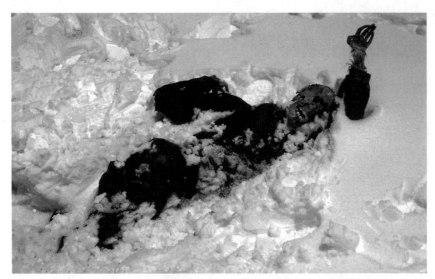

Unidentified mummified corpse in the glacier snow at the foot of Annapurna I

acting as if it had nothing to do with us, we slipped by and continued our climb. We carried on, the dead man was dead, and there was nothing more we could do to help him. We wasted no time puzzling over who he might once have been, or how he had died. After all, several dozen people had perished on Annapurna, perhaps even more than had thus far reached the summit of this eight-thousander.

Hours later, Hans and I looked around for a safe place to set up camp. We had to find a bivouac site before the swirling snow made it impossible to see where we were going.

Hans, a mountain guide from the Ahrntal in South Tyrol, and in those days still very young, was eager to get a move on. Since setting off from Base Camp in the early hours of morning, to study the "Normal Route" that had become such a trap for the French party in 1950, we had penetrated deeper and deeper into a wilderness. Here, there was no zone that was without objective dangers. This glacier world, invisible from below, now appeared to us as an endless chaos.

By midday the mists creeping up the mountainsides from the narrow defile of the Miristi Khola had caught up with us, then enveloped us completely; often we could see no more than 6 feet (2 m) ahead. The whiteout caused the chaotic jumble of ice to shrink and grow continually. Would a descent of the French Route be at all possible under such conditions? Who could tell?

And so we waited it out. We decided to pitch a tent and bivouac.

Although this was expedition-style mountaineering we were doing in those days, and, compared to the Alpine sport climbing of later years, a kind

*Annapurna Northwest
Face. Directly above the
bergschrund, the ice was
vertical.*

of relic from a long-forgotten age, the Himalayas still offered many more
options than in earlier times. The "last great problems" on the eight-
thousanders—the big faces, ridges, and buttresses—represented similar
challenges to the routes established almost 100 years ago in the Alps by the
likes of Zsigmondy, Dibona, and Preuss. Only the scale was different,
the dangers too, and the feeling of being out there alone and reliant on one's
own skill and judgment. Indeed, it was this feeling of exposure that remained
the most important criterion for the greatness of a climb.

Even if the Himalayas had meanwhile become a "black patch on the
map"—surveyed, explored, and described in detail—they were still there for
anyone to rediscover who wished to do so. Those little groups of climbers,
male and female, who were prepared to take the trouble to identify new
lines and then to climb them with limited resources and limited artificial
aids experienced Annapurna or K2 in exactly the same way as the pioneers
had done.

Because it was so easy to lose one's way at such great altitudes, it was
also crucial, I felt, to get to know the whole massif of an eight-thousander
before you set off on the climb. The climber who merely concentrated his
studies on one segment of the mountain he had come to climb could easily
have become a prisoner of his own courage, commitment, and ambition.

The weather the following morning was good, as is usual before sunrise. We observed the huge North Face of Annapurna and stored the images in our memories, as if these pictures might later become necessary for our very survival. Then, brimming with confidence, we returned to Base Camp.

While Hans and I had been studying the French Route on the North Face, Reinhard Patscheider, Reinhard Schiestl, and Prem Darshano had progressed a good way up the Northwest Face, fixing ropes and getting a first impression of the scale of this eight-thousander. These Himalayan newcomers had thus proved that they were not only skillful climbers but also had stamina and commitment.

When they came down for a few days' rest, Hans and I set off up the face. Just above Camp I, which we had established a week previously, the rock and ice steepened alarmingly. From below, the Northwest Face of Annapurna appeared so grim and forbidding that it was not only our ultimate success on the route that was called into question—even making an attempt seemed a gruesome proposition. With each upward glance, even the thought of setting off up the route was a frightening prospect. Each of us felt the same; from farther down, the face appeared to be possible, but at the foot of the wall, we hesitated about making a start. As Hans and I stood in the large cirque below the steep face, listening to the avalanches of stones that

The first 3,300 feet (1000 m) of the Northwest Face of Annapurna are at an angle of 60–70 degrees.

Steep ice climbing just below the second high camp on the Northwest Face of Annapurna

Camp I, protected by an ice bulge, was a good distance from the start of the climb.

Traverse to Camp II in the huge corner system at midheight on the face

thunder down in the afternoons, shaking the concave section at the base of the wall with their impact, we exchanged worried glances.

Nevertheless, we at least had to try. And anyway, we had left a backdoor open—in the event that the first ascent of the huge, concave Northwest Face should go wrong, or that our courage should finally prove insufficient, there was always the much easier route that Herzog's team had found. We would establish Camp II first, reconnoiter the second third of the face, and then decide.

Right from the start, Hans and I climbed together. We belonged together, and we formed one of two teams, an arrangement that was to remain until the end of the expedition. The fact that the other three considered themselves to be the second team was neither intended, nor was it particularly helpful for our progress on the route. Unfortunately, this situation soon led to tensions, which remained unspoken. There was a rivalry between the two teams, a rivalry that existed right up until the journey home.

It is true that we climbers often compete with each other. Those from town A compete with those from town B, Smith against Jones, neighbor versus neighbor. But on Annapurna it was all a matter of combining our

Camp II, at about 19,700 feet (6000 m)

ideas, strength, and courage to climb the route. These little power games and overt competitiveness soon sap all your energy. We would not have gotten very far like that. Despite being aware of the consequences, however, I was unable to unite the two teams.

Hans and I climbed the first quarter of the face prepared by our companions, until we were at a height of about 19,600 feet (6000 m). There, in the shelter of a lateral crevasse, we pitched a small tent and set about arranging our 10 square feet (3 sq m) of space to bivouac for the night. When packing our rucksacks the following morning, Hans insisted that we take everything with us, including all the gear and food, for a possible summit push. It was clever thinking.

I naturally asked myself whether we would have the slightest chance of getting to the summit by such a difficult route this early in the year, but gave in to the youngster's hassling without protest. While packing the sacks, I was briefly visited by that old fear rising from the subconscious, a fear that, despite the numerous ascents I have made on the eight-thousanders, I have never quite managed to shake. What had we let ourselves in for? What might happen up there?

On the smooth rock band in the central part of the face, one of the crux sections of the climb

It was not just the objective dangers—lightning strike and snowstorm, rockfall and avalanche—that might hinder our progress. Above all it was my own weaknesses that frightened me. I had experienced this feeling of hopelessness at the end of the world so often that I now had difficulty in putting it to the back of my mind. The fear did not diminish with increased experience; it became greater year by year. And with every new expedition, it grew more and more difficult to bite the bullet and go for it, to set off for just one more attempt.

Face your fear and do it anyway—Hans was right. Perhaps it was now, and only now, that we would get those few days of fine weather that would make such a difficult and dangerous first ascent possible. Whether such a risk was justifiable was another matter entirely, but the possibility excited us, and it was this that provided the challenge. We were both ready to move now, and prepared to give it our best shot, but we knew that we would only be successful if we were in top form and the conditions and the timing were exactly right. Hans, in his youthful, carefree way, had been the first to feel it and he simply said, "Let's give it a try."

It was only when we started climbing that I regained my composure. I concentrated only on the next move, on the days to come, on the mountain.

It was April 22. We had left our bivouac tent in the gray light of dawn and climbed unroped, up snowfields at first, then smooth ice, to reach a smooth rock band in the middle of the face that looked more than a little unfriendly. At first we hesitated, then we roped up and finally overcame it by a series of delicate traverses to the right. This was friction climbing at 21,300 feet (6500 m), hands and feet pressed flat against the rock!

For a short time we climbed directly upward below huge seracs, our breath coming in short gasps, to reach safe ground above. This section was so exposed that the view down between our legs made the glacier at the foot of the face look quite flat; the drop was breathtaking. The wall broke away 6,000 feet (almost 2000 m) below us, while above was just the black abyss of the sky. Somewhere between the two we clung to the wall, between rock, ice, and a few stray tatters of mist blown in from the west by the sharp wind.

We had not noticed how quickly the day was darkening. We were already above the big, vertical serac on the upper concave section of the face when suddenly we climbed straight into the driving, windblown snow. All sense of direction was lost; the only thing we could see were little gray patches, ill-defined slopes somewhere above us. Another whiteout. Occasional flashes of sunlight pierced the swirling mists like the beam of a spotlight.

We were now climbing directly upward again. Why weren't we going down? We wanted to find a spot to bivouac and to do that, we had to get up higher. Below a pointed tower of ice, we managed to seek out a piece of flat ground a hand's breadth in size and set to work hacking the ice away on the mountain side of the slope. It took us hours to flatten out a space big enough for the tent.

And so we sat there, trapped by the typical Annapurna weather. There was no question of either descending or climbing on up. Even the few feet (meters) from our bivy site to the ice tower seemed an insurmountable prospect.

The storm was raging even before we had the tent up. As an emergency measure, we anchored the flapping cloth, threw the gear inside, and crawled into the tiny tent. Without its protection, we would have rapidly become hypothermic. Crouching out in the open on the face, in the teeth of the storm, we would not have been able to hold out until morning. And with no visibility, it was impossible to make a move; we would have been unable to feel our way, either up or down. We would have been lost, even though there were two of us. We felt safe in the tent, but what if the fabric should tear?

The wind was so strong that we could no longer make ourselves understood, so we refrained from talking. It was as if there were no longer any communication between us, even face to face. So we waited for an improvement in the weather and, with it, a chance to descend.

Hours like these stay in your memory. The accompanying images may only occupy a space of 6 square feet (2 sq m), yet the feeling of exposure, of being lost, at the time almost unbearable, remains, and can be recalled at will at any time, even years later.

In the tent, perched on a narrow ledge between a leaning tower of ice, a crevasse, and the abyss, we waited until the worst was over. Suddenly everything went quiet; all that could be heard now was the distant thunder and the hiss of the avalanches. We began to doze.

It was getting toward evening, about five o'clock, when the lightning and thunder drew closer again. Perhaps an hour had passed since the last roll of thunder when suddenly the sky was lit by bolts of lightning. With every close strike, we instinctively ducked. And so we went on: reacting, waiting, listening intently, until things became quiet again outside. Both of us cowered quietly in our sleeping bags, neither wishing to tell the other just what it was he was thinking about.

Meanwhile, it had gotten dark. But it was only hours later that tiredness and cold made me so apathetic that I was able to suppress thoughts of the dangers outside the tent. We even managed to sleep fitfully, and gradually the night passed in dozing and waiting.

On the morning of April 23—a miracle had happened!—the weather was fine again. So onward and upward! We climbed another 1,200 feet (350 m) higher, up shimmering blue ice, rock slabs, and finally on snow, and bivouacked again between a rock ledge and a wall of ice.

The afternoon again brought high winds. Again we lay in our sleeping bags and waited, each of us completely silent, while the walls of the tent flapped in the wind. Although we had our eyes shut and were trying hard to put a dampener on all of our senses during the long night, the fear remained. To be frightened and to be thinking at the same time costs you a lot of energy, so I tried at least to avoid any further thought. Surely we could dispense with caution in the tent at least? So, turning the flame of life down low for a while, we dozed the night away.

There was no moonlight, yet even at four o'clock in the morning it was so light that you did not need a flashlight to see in the tent. Maybe at 24,600 feet (7500 m) above sea level the snow on the glacier was reflecting back the morning sky in the east?

When we stepped out of the tent into the gray light of dawn, it was very cold and still quite dark. Up above the summit ridge a clear day was dawning, and there was hardly any wind.

Should we carry on? Why not. The steep ice and dark rock between us and the heavens still looked like relics from outer space and the roaring was still to be heard high above our heads, but that was all a long way away. The wind was still blasting over the summit ridge with such force that whole chunks of snow were being sent flying through the air. But on the face itself there was dead calm. So we went on.

The northwest wind has been hammering against this steep mountain face for millions of years; since the Himalayas were formed, cold and high winds have been a part of life up here.

But would the storm-force winds up on the summit ridge abate? That was the big worry. Still, the storm was not catastrophic—not yet, not as long as we did not have to climb right into it. In any case, catastrophes are invented by us humans, and no one had forced us to come up here.

On the one hand, it appeared to me that we were only there by coincidence; on the other hand, there was something in me that rejected the idea of retreating off the route. In spite of this, the doubts and fears remained. Why was it that we wished to continue? Was our behavior up there irrational? Or is it as the critics presume, that once we get too close to the summit, it is the subconscious mind that decides was has to happen next.

How certain Hans now was as he climbed the glassy-smooth sheet of ice directly above the bivy tent, and in temperatures so deep into the minus figures! He was dancing up the vertical ice. It was all so absurd that I could not even shake my head in amazement. But his decisiveness was infectious, and I found myself being drawn in. It took away some of my fear. And the ridge above seemed so unrealistically near that suddenly we found ourselves climbing faster. Maybe it was because we just wanted to get onto the other side and get the view from there.

But once on the summit ridge, we were out of the lee side and were suddenly standing in the teeth of the gale, in the danger zone. We stood between the swelling banks of fog on the south side of the ridge and the windblown spindrift on the north side, braced against the wind and potential disaster. From this position the valleys to the south looked unreal, and so far below; the glaciers were a silky gray color; the sharp edges of the rocks up ahead stood out like black sculptures scattered between the patches of ice.

Presently the world began to appear and disappear piece by piece through the tatters of mist that blew in. Where were we? How high? Was rescue a possibility? And if so, how? No, the consequences of an accident were now no longer to be contemplated. Our senses were dulled, we had lost all sense of perspective.

Like the summit ridge of Dhaulagiri, which we climbed a little later, the final ridge on Annapurna is very exposed to the wind.

The face to the right of the summit ridge is almost vertical. The snow was sticking to the south side, the side we were in danger of falling down if the wind were to drop suddenly. The rock crumbled when we grabbed hold of it; it was not good-quality rock at all. The ice splintered under our crampons; it was not good ice either. The lumps of snow we kicked loose and the handholds we broke off were immediately torn away by the wind.

From time to time the sun made an appearance, but it had no power. The pale light and the clouds, loose swirls of mist and vague patches of light dancing on the broken rocks far below, lent our world something ethereal. And from the west a new bank of mist came in, piles of gloomy fog, more and more of it, filling the Kali-Gandaki. A wedge of cloud boiling up from below violently pushed the last remains of the blue sky apart.

Hans and I were still climbing, following the line of the ridge with brief detours to the left or right, keeping to the lee side wherever possible. But the howling wind was still making itself heard. The sounds we were making— our breathing, the bright ring of the pick of the ax when it struck rock—were lost amid this all-encompassing noise, a roaring, rushing sound like an underground train passing through a station. When the mists parted, it was painfully bright and the pinnacles and towers above us stood sharply silhouetted against the blue-black background of the sky like paper cutouts before disappearing into the murky clouds again.

Later on, on a long snow arête—we were still a good way below the summit—our little world suddenly brightened up, possibly because the abyss to the left and right was filled with dense mists, and we had views like those out of an airplane window! But there was still the cold and the fear of falling to contend with, together with the feeling of hopelessness one has on such a huge mountain. We were so slow.

After dealing with two difficult steep pitches—first a 50-foot (15-m) rock step, then an ice wall over on the south side—we mostly climbed without protection, moving together. Yet even without textbook running belays, we still took an eternity, it seemed, to reach the next rock ledge up. Luckily the snow was hard and I was generally able to follow in Hans' footsteps, but when we met up again to feel our way gingerly along just below the crest of the summit ridge, keeping on the lee side between the rocks and hard snow, we often did not have much idea what we were doing.

We had studied "our" face and the West Ridge for weeks on end, and both of us had imprinted the line of our route on our memory. We thought that we knew every single feature, like the details of a picture. Viewed from below, it was just like a postcard, but now all we could make out were sections of this ridge, perched up there between the clouds, and occasional glimpses of the summit, or what we thought was the summit. And big chasms everywhere! In addition there was that ever-present high wind, as if we were trapped in a wind tunnel. Of the image we had of the mountain, the one we had stored in our memory and had pieced together in our mind's eye from a thousand tiny mosaic pieces, there was nothing more to be seen—just that edge of snow, your partner, the slopes of ice and bits of rock that, luckily, were no longer vertical.

Looking down the South Face made me feel dizzy. The fact that the colossal chunks of rock, perched precariously out at an angle, had not fallen down defied all nature's laws. With a shudder of horror, I saw where Whillans and Haston had climbed up back in 1970. It was just a steep, bottomless pit down there!

Hans gave the impression of being nice and relaxed. When he was reaching up for the next handholds or leaning around a corner to find the continuation of the route, he was totally focused. When taking a rest, he just slumped down onto his ice ax, leaning onto it and catching his breath, taking great lungfuls of air. Climbing with Hans gave you a feeling of hope and belief in yourself. We knew each other well, trusted each other, worked well as a team.

We kept in radio contact with Base Camp, calling in at frequent intervals, but otherwise there was no help at all from anyone else. In the same way as I managed to glean certain pieces of information from the fragments of words emanating from the radio equipment, I later took a few pictures with the camera—all of it done on autopilot, as it were. It was as if our only

Annapurna I, 26,545 feet (8091 m), in high winds: Hans Kammerlander leans against the summit ridge.

link with the world was through these pieces of technical equipment. "A competiton for survival" is how Hans Kammerlander later described our situation.

Why was it that I was always looking around? What was I looking for? There had never been anyone up there! "Never been anyone up here," I said to myself. Up here it was even hard to imagine God's existence. I perceived this dead world as being not only no place for humankind, the exposure too hung like a question mark in my mind. Yes, quite apart from the security afforded by the rope, I found myself wishing for a higher power to protect me.

My feet had been without feeling for hours now, and again and again I felt the chunks of snow on my face whipped up by the gale out of the tracks in front of me. Hans Kammerlander again: "It was like someone was belting me in the face with a wire brush." With eyes wide open and mouths agape, we finally arrived at the top. Once on the summit, our pain evaporated briefly, or was it that it had merely passed beyond endurance? The fear, however, remained.

It was a little after eleven o'clock when we suddenly found ourselves standing on top of the firm dome of snow, staring at each other. Like two men on the run. We stood there, shivering, a little bit proud, yet at the same time still with a feeling of urgency, for we knew that in order to fully appreciate this success, we would first have to get back down, back to safety. So we experienced none of the usual disappointment on the summit.

We could not see much from the summit. Machapuchare appeared for a brief moment from behind a gray veil of mist, there were tatters of blue sky and Hans' ice-encrusted face. A huge bank of clouds hung before and above Dhaulagiri. Like an island. Only once did the wind tear a hole in the clouds, long enough for us to see right down to Base Camp, but we could make nothing out. Tents, moraines, and glaciers formed a single gray mass.

The weather was visibly deteriorating. Which way down? The summit was still shrouded in light clouds. It would not now be possible to find the route of the first ascent party. So it had to be back down the way we had come, down-climb the route—there was no other choice.

Hans had been the one who had forced the issue, made this summit push work, right up to the last stretch of the climb; it was he who had done the routefinding and he who had rammed his ice ax again and again into the snow in front of me—he had been the driving force, and he remained so. Hans, coiled like an animal ready to spring throughout this expedition, was prepared for the risky descent. In the final instance, it was his decisiveness that we had to thank for our success on Annapurna and his instincts that helped us in our escape back down to the valley. We had taken the only chance we had to go for an early summit push, we had climbed the difficult sections quickly, and so we had time in reserve for the descent.

The Northwest Face of Annapurna I: descent through spindrift

On the way back down, I first had to get used to looking down the whole time. Although we could often see only as far as the next cluster of rocks, we knew that it went down step by step. Twice we had to rappel, once on the ridge and once down to the south. The void below seemed bottomless. The constant fear of making a mistake remained unspoken between us; we moved in silence, and this silence also helped us come to terms with the fact that the descent was a long one, very long. We were not always able stick to the ridge itself; at one stage we had to leave it for the face on the right, gaining it via a gully, and then make another detour to bypass a rock tower on the left. The wind here was so strong that it was as if we were weightless; we had to hold on to each other to stop ourselves from being torn from the ridge.

As long as we were climbing down, the exhaustion worked like a kind of opium on our tired bodies. I was aware, however, that at all costs we must not sit down to take a rest. We would never have gotten to our feet again. I have no idea what we were thinking as we reached the foot of the steep summit ridge. Nothing, probably. Just continue down! Staying up there was, in any case, out of the question. The wind was so strong in the vicinity of the ridge, and snow was boiling up from below. Beside us was the narrow snow arête; below us, smooth, cream-colored slabs of rock. Gasping for breath, we trudged back uphill for a little way in order to descend from the shoulder onto the Northwest Face. Midday had come and gone, and the air was full of the promise of storms and more fresh falls of snow, but we could not have climbed any faster. The tips of our fingers and the soles of our feet had been devoid of any feeling for so long now that I no longer felt the cold. I had to look at what I was touching to make sure I could hang onto it. The worst thing now was the fear of the imminent snowfall, and the attendant dangers of avalanche and of getting lost or stuck up there.

I was now hearing voices more and more often, together with a repeated screeching sound as my crampons slipped on the rocky slabs. It could not be the other members of our expedition; we were only expecting to see Reinhard Patscheider and Reinhard Schiestl in the late afternoon.

The hours passed quickly. As the mists grew thicker and the sun broke through less and less frequently, evening came. We were now descending on the double rope, down-climbing the mirror-smooth ice pitch that Hans had led free in the morning, and soon came across our bivy tent, which we dismantled and packed up in no time at all. Which way down now? The rocky outcrops below us on the face grew and diminished in the changing light, sometimes bathed in an eerie glow, sometimes deep in shadows. No, this face was not made for men. But we were there anyway, and I was having the strangest thoughts. Not fantasies about being all-powerful, but thoughts of being rewarded by fate. But what does that prove?

We still needed to take all our gear back down with us, just in case. You never knew. So we crammed stoves, the tent, and sleeping bags into our rucksacks. We only had a small amount of hardware with us: just three titanium ice screws, a few slings, two rock pegs, and two lengths of rope, one 50

Reinhard Patscheider descending through the snowstorm. His sure, safe way of moving was unmistakable.

feet (15 m) and the other 100 feet (30 m) long. We had to abandon the short rope just below the bivy site, where we also had to sacrifice one of the pitons. We reached a roof of snow via a rock ledge; this was where we had waited out the storm two days earlier.

Again, we had to search for the route; there was nothing more to be seen of our old tracks. Luckily we found the ice tower that had already provided us with shelter once before. It split the mists apart in a weird, ghostly sort of way. Thereafter, there were no further points of reference; we just headed straight down the fall line to the upper band of seracs, which stuck out from the 9,800-foot (3000-m) face like a huge balcony. We continued on down for hours on end, faces to the wall, placing our crampons alternately, feeling our way cautiously, never resting on one foot for more than a few seconds at a time.

It was the fear of darkness that now drove us on, coupled with the ever-present risk of avalanches and rockfall. The salvos of stones that clattered down into the snow to our left and right could just have easily hit us, but in the fog and spindrift, the danger could only be heard and not seen. If we had been able to see the stones coming, the fear would have been less sharp, but in the semidarkness, every whir and hum represented a possible direct hit. And as it grew darker, so the danger and the fear grew.

At last a tiny figure appeared in the snow gully far below. It was Reinhard Patscheider, "Bagger" to his friends. He was carrying a rope and climbing fast. When we met up with him on the band of snow beneath the smooth sweep of slabs, we could see that he had exhausted himself.

Patscheider was too short of breath and probably far too excited to ask us any questions, and we were too tired to thank him. The simple fact that

Rappelling down the steep face. During the snowstorm, Reinhard Patscheider assumed responsibility, and after meeting up with Messner and Kammerlander, it was he who went as last man on the rappels.

he was there worked like a drug. Help meant security, confidence; it gave us renewed strength.

Patscheider had voluntarily put himself in this dangerous situation just to help us; it was a selfless gesture. However, there were many other supposedly "selfless" climbers whom I had met who acted out of rather more suspect motives. They required nothing else of themselves beyond the pretense of being special in some way. They conducted themselves like heroes whenever they were within striking distance of whoever was in need of rescue. It was always a case of "saving a comrade's life." However, this had not been the case with Lachenal, nor was it applicable to Patscheider. It was just obvious to him to act as he had done.

So now we were three. At first we just stood and stared at each other. Then, as previously arranged by radio, Reinhard tied his rope off and we climbed down it hand over hand. Now and then, little snow avalanches went sloughing down past us, and when we pulled the rope, down from somewhere came the tinkle of ice splinters. Farther down, a few rocks came leaping past and one of them caught me on the left knee. I watched with eyes wide open as a few larger lumps disappeared into the void with giant leaps. Of course it was wrong to descend this gully in new snow and at night, but it was a mistake we could no longer correct.

With Reinhard Patscheider as the driving force, Reinhard Schiestl as the cool, calculating one, and Prem Darshano as the hesitant member of the team, the three-man rope set off up the face once more. They got to just below the vertical barrier of cliffs below the summit ridge before turning back. During the descent, Patscheider stepped into a hole in the snow, lost his footing, and fell nearly 1,300 feet (400 m). The fact that he survived is nothing short of a miracle.

Annapurna Northwest Face. Traversing the avalanche-prone slope on the descent from the middle concave section of the face to the tents of Camp II

Descending over the bergschrund at the foot of the Northwest Face of Annapurna: the end of the dangers

We tried as far as possible to avoid the bed of the huge corner system when descending. Volleys of stones had scoured a deep trench in the middle of the gully and all the snow collected in it, only to slide off again at regular intervals. We kept to the right and left of it as we climbed down by the light of our headlamps. It went on forever.

Our situation was critical. We now had Reinhard Schiestl to show us the way down, but we were still in an area very prone to avalanches. If we managed to get to Camp II we would survive, despite the snowstorm. Below that, there were fixed ropes on the face, luckily.

The snow in the gully came to an abrupt end. One of the two Reinhards tied a rope off to his ice ax and lowered it over the last steep step. I no longer knew if I was the one giving the instructions, just that they stayed above while Hans and I hand-over-handed down the rope. A signal was given, they untied the rope, and it came snaking down to us. Our helpers soloed down this last section of the climb before the camp and soon caught up with us. Then the four of us waded through the deep snow to the snow-covered tents of Camp II. We were saved! At least for now.

What now followed was a night without sleep, our fitful attempts to nod off constantly interrupted by slides of snow that pattered on the fabric of the tents, by the shouts of our friends who were frightened of suffocating, and by the dull footsteps of Patscheider who spent the time from ten o'clock until the following morning shoveling the tents free of snow over and over again.

Alone in my tent—Hans had dug himself a snow hole with Reinhard Schiestl—with the weight of the snow pressing down on me, it felt like I was

Prem Darshano, an excellent rock climber, is the only surviving member of the second team. Schiestl died as a result of a car accident, while Patscheider lost his life in the mountains.

lying in my own grave. Life outside would go on without me, I thought, so I tried to catch some sleep and forget all my worries. And this "outside" seemed so far away now and in a way uninteresting. The next day, with Reinhard Patscheider's help, I managed to free myself from the tent, and in spite of the avalanche danger we all went down to Base Camp.

The wall of a thousand fears and sorrows loomed frighteningly large at the head of the valley as we made our way to Dhaulagiri a few weeks later. We had done the Northwest Face of Annapurna, "cracked it," as we climbers are wont to say when we manage to climb a route. And the dangers were soon forgotten; no, not forgotten, but forced into the background, denigrated as being banal. Yet here was Hans Kammerlander, taking a last look back at Annapurna and noting, "After a big route in the Alps, I always think I know myself, know exactly who I am. It is only above 26,000 feet (8000 m) that I realize again and again just how little I really do know about myself and my body, myself and the mountain."

FROM THE WEST-NORTHWEST

Annapurna I (far left), the Shoulder (Sans Nom), and The Fang, viewed from the north. The Czech Route takes a line up the ice rib to the left of the Sans Nom Buttress (French Route) to the Shoulder itself, and then climbs the West Ridge to the Main Summit.

WEST RIDGE/ NORTH FACE ROUTE TO THE SHOULDER 1988

The first ascent of Annapurna from the west, done in 1988, was a fine and difficult achievement, yet one that gained little recognition in international mountaineering circles. It is not a route that I propose to ignore in this anthology, however. Josef Nežerka, one of the men to reach the summit, kindly allowed me to make use of the report he wrote of his experiences, and it is with reference to this report that I intend to portray what happened back in 1988.

Nežerka, a climber from Bohemia in the former Eastern Bloc, had grown up on the local sandstone and earned his living as a building site laborer, working without scaffolding on the roofs of houses or high-rise buildings. In those days, work of this sort enabled many climbers to finance their expeditions to Poland, Czechoslovakia, Hungary, and Slovenia. Included in their ranks were many of the finest high-altitude mountaineers around, men like Josef Nežerka.

In 1988 the objective was Annapurna. First of all, there was the journey there to consider. Then Nepal. "Katmandu came and went," Nežerka wrote, briefly and succinctly.

Most of the members of the expedition had already acclimatized with an ascent of Kang Tegri in the Tien Shan range. Moreover, they nearly all knew each other, and the whole trip became one big shared experience: "just us, the mountains, and the unavoidable high-altitude vomiting."

One evening on the approach, Annapurna was suddenly revealed; it was such a threatening sight that they were all shaken. "After a terrible day's walk, what now appeared out of the black clouds and the thin sleet was sheer horror. It was all going to the dogs; we too, absolutely drained. We don't know where we are, we don't know why we are here or even who we are. We only know that we are all so terribly small and insignificant. I just hope to God it lets us live for a little while longer."

The image lasted just a few seconds, yet it stunned the climbers into paralysis. "We could hardly manage to take photographs, then darkness fell once more. Fang and Annapurna. No, I never did want to climb The Fang! Some of the group rolled into camp late into the night; they were scared, but not as scared as we were—we had seen it."

The next day, in the bright light of morning, with tall grass and rocks in the foreground that reminded Josef Nežerka of gravestones, the mountain range nevertheless looked splendid.

Base Camp was low down and the route to the foot of the face was dangerous. "Everyone in the group is working perfectly well together, the old, the young, and even the very young. It's all very pleasing; I like it. Even the logistics, and the searching for a possible line."

The camp at the foot of the face, a kind of Advanced Base Camp, was not ideally situated. "It wasn't I who chose the spot," Nežerka said, "I didn't like it; everything was kind of hanging over the edge. I didn't really want to sleep there, but had to, I guess. And it was a horrible night. There is nothing worse than having to sit in your tent, waiting to see if an avalanche is going to come down or not. All you want to do is leap out to somehow avoid the danger of seeing it."

Afterward they repositioned the camp, and the original site was later hit by several avalanches. Two of the three Japanese who had been climbing not far from my 1985 route were killed by the pressure wave of an avalanche just like these. "So the spot was not a good one. It is worthwhile listening to

In the icefall beneath the North Face of Annapurna I, a collection point for avalanches

one's intuition. After all, a good camp is the key to survival, a place to rest and find new strength." How right Josef Nežerka is. The camp must be a place for calm relaxation, a place to sleep, to rest and think things over.

"The West Face offers everything a climb can offer a climber, and all of it leads continually upward. There is humility, when you are almost running below the seracs in order to spend as little time there as possible; trust, when you make promises, cling to your hopes, believe in your expectations—and luck is with you; excitement, in the steep ice chimneys, often wading up to your waist through snow that no one has touched before you; the joy of movement, in the coordination of your body on rock and ice; strength, when you are standing on the front points of your crampons for hours on end, hanging on to your ice ax and making your way up vertical pitches of ice. You worry about the bad weather, the wind, the avalanches, your own mistakes, and your own shortcomings, including the responsibility for your climbing partners. You concentrate on the steep sections, climbing at the very limit of what is justifiable without adequate protection. Then there are your private thoughts in the long hours, when it is no longer a matter of making this or that mistake and you have enough time to reflect on the meaning of it all; the tension about making the right decisions about when to set off, what to take, which line to choose, who to climb with, and when you should turn back."

After establishing a camp at 23,300 feet (7100 m), they fixed a short section above the camp and three of them set off for the summit: Nežerka, Jirka Pelikán, and Jindřich Martiš. They managed to push their route to just below the West Shoulder, dubbed the "Sans Nom" by the French, at about 25,600 feet (7800 m). "And now the three of us are sitting at a col below Sans Nom. It is half past one in the afternoon and we won't make it to the top today. Ahead of us lies the knife-edged, heavily featured crest of a ridge, a few steep upsweeps, and farther on a big protruding block of rock split by an ice gully; hopefully this won't stop us dead in our tracks. We are still not thinking about the endless slog up to the summit; for the moment it is leaving me in peace."

Josef knew that they might not make it. Nevertheless, he approved Jindra and Jirka's strategy for a "super-lightweight push." In the morning, however, he added a few little items to the day's equipment they had agreed to carry: a stove, their smallest gas bottle, and some tea and sugar. They intended to move together, unroped. "I can carry that lot easily. With gloves, food, and a 65-foot (20-m) length of Kevlar rope, the rucksack is not too heavy anyway."

Jindra asked Josef to take a shovel. A snow trench is not a tent, but 3 feet (a meter) of snow was lying everywhere and the bivouac equipment was too heavy for such a long stretch. Nežerka, Martiš, and Pelikán were now ready to move.

Josef Nežerka, the strongest mountaineer on the 1988 Czech Expedition

The three of them felt great as they set off on October 11. After more than 8 hours' climbing, they reached the col between Annapurna and Sans Nom, at an altitude of about 25,600 feet (7800 m), arriving there within about 10 minutes of each other. The descent would present no problems, they thought, because they had not needed the rope on the way up. Josef Nežerka was the first to get to the col. The biting cold soon got him moving again.

"I am freezing now and wandering about trying to find the route. I hand-traverse the crest of the ridge—exciting stuff. Below my feet is the couloir taken by the Messner Route—an almost vertical wall, dropping sheer below me. It's blowing a gale, the wind howling horribly. A little way behind me I can now see Jindra; he's moving again now as well. It is so cold that I have to keep climbing. Things are going well, until I suddenly catch sight of a 50-foot- (15-m-) high rock step, shaped like a head, blocking the way. Will it go? I squeeze through a fissure in the rock, through to the southern side of the ridge, and there find Paradise: warmth, no wind at all, and a wall of ice that is vertical but climbable."

Meanwhile, what had happened to his friends? For a while Josef enjoyed the warmth, then started to worry about wasting time and continued on his way. "So I tie in to the rope and try to climb very carefully. For a time everything goes OK, but then the snow, gnawed at by the sun, starts to get soft. It is hard work just to go one step. And time is running out. Suddenly Jindra appears."

"Where is Jirka?" Josef asked.

"Jirka decided to turn back," Jindra said.

"I left the rucksack down there."

Josef hammered in a piton. The snow was better here and he managed to reach a second steepening in the ridge, a little way below the "Head."

By the time Josef had climbed the pitch and Jindra had come up to join him, it was already late. A bivouac, then. It was no longer very far to the top, but it was rapidly growing dark. They had a splendid view across to Dhaulagiri, and over the South Summit of Annapurna to the Nepalese countryside beyond. The weather was good.

They took a few photos and then quickly started digging, first a channel and then, parallel to the crest of the ridge, a wider trench, fashioning a snow cave for themselves with thick walls like a tent. Only when it was completely dark did they crawl inside and seal the entrance with blocks of ice.

"So we sit there drinking ice-cold water and eating a bit of food. We think about Jirka; he must have arrived back at the camp by now. We envy him his tent and sleeping bag; experience has taught us that the nights up here can be very long and get very cold. In fact we can only sit upright, wriggle around from side to side as we try to catch some sleep. We take turns falling over one another and generally make a nuisance of ourselves. It's claustrophobic in here. Every time we try to shift position, stand up, stamp some life back into our feet, or massage our knotted muscles, we manage to get on each other's nerves."

Soon they could sleep no more, teeth chattering with the cold. "I now play my trump card—the stove. Jindra grunts with pleasure. After a cup of warm water, we doze a little until we get cold again."

More teeth chattering. The stove is lit again. Another round of warm water. And back to waiting.

"The side walls of our 'tent' suddenly begin to grow lighter. In spite of this, we haven't the slightest inclination to crawl out of our hole. Outside there is a wild wind whistling and it's crazy cold. With frozen mouths, we choke down some cheese and some other nice stuff, longing to be able to move quickly again."

Once they were outside, everything started to go much better. "It took a long time before we got a bit more mobile. Neither the gully splitting the 'Head' nor the blunt ridge leading to the summit are particularly challenging from a climbing point of view, but we rope up nevertheless. The ridge is just fearsomely long. After every bump, another one appears; and since each one looks a little higher than the last, we continue to plod on upward. Dull and lifeless and out of breath, I suddenly look up. As soon as I have caught my breath, I see that the ground beneath me is sloping gently downward. So I look back. Same thing in that direction. We are on the top!"

Jindřich Martiš and Josef Nežerka had thus accomplished a long and

Jindřich Martiš just a few feet (meters) below the summit of Annapurna I

difficult route, combining two established routes to achieve their first ascent—a fine effort! It was just a shame that Jirka Pelikán had decided to turn back.

Josef pulled out his camera and took a snapshot of Jindra climbing up toward him with Dhaulagiri in the background. He had a bit of a soft spot for that distant mountain: "It was over there that in 1985, storm-force winds almost swept us away just as we had finished climbing the whole face."

The two friends' enjoyment of the high point of their Annapurna climb was short-lived; the descent would certainly be no easy matter.

"Jindra is deeply moved by the experience. He even cried. 'After all these years I've finally managed it. Thanks for dragging me up here.' It is his first eight-thousander. Mine too."

Josef, who was every bit as emotional, said, "I am happy that I'm up here with you. It's a shame Jirka turned back." They chatted away, grimacing with the pain, took some more photographs, and tried to videotape.

The two men had no flags or banners with them, so there was no flag-waving and no victory poses. Their precipitous departure had surprised even them, and they had given no thought to any ceremonies. Nor was there any feeling of duty. In any case, it was now windy and cold. Soon they fled the summit and started the descent.

The descent went well; they knew the way, of course. Down at the grotto camp, they collected their rucksacks again and then rappelled down the difficult steep section. It wasn't long before they were back at the col between Annapurna I and Sans Nom.

"Jindra, look," said Josef, "do you see the tracks leading up to Sans Nom?"

It all became clear now. Jirka had not gone back down straight away; he

Behind and parallel to the first rock arête is the line of the Czech Route, which follows the sharp West Ridge behind the Peak Sans Nom (West Shoulder) to the Main Summit.

had probably told himself he could climb another peak on the day of his daughter's birthday.

"Yes, that's what he said to me, and Sans Nom is only 1,000 feet or so (a few hundred meters) from here," Josef thought. An hour perhaps, he calculated. "The crafty old dog!"

Josef and Jindra hurried on down; the thought of a tent, a sleeping bag, and some warm food gave them wings.

"We lose height quickly. After a while we get to a ramp that cuts across the rock walls below Sans Nom."

The terrain got steeper now; below them was a 230-foot- (70-m-) high vertical wall. It was a dangerous place; they could not afford to make any mistakes here. Josef was just thinking it might be better to rappel when he caught sight of an ice ax, one of Jirka's gloves, an ice peg, and a length of Kevlar rope. Surely it could not be? Had Jirka slipped and fallen?

A horrified shudder ran through Josef. "I grab everything, hammer in an ice peg, tie off the rope, and wait for Jindra. We do not speak, even though I feel like screaming. But there is nothing to say. We can just hope. Maybe he is already back at camp. So we race on down and I dive into the tent—he is not there. And he never was there. Presently, Jindra arrives; he looks at me. I shake my head. We race farther down. He is not at the second camp either. Only Zuzanna is there, Zuzanna the old mountain warrior. I had climbed the Messner Route on the Northwest Face of the Civetta in winter with her—10 days of hell on Earth it was."

At the bergschrund—time to breathe again. But just below lay the body of Jirka Pelikán.

There could be no doubt about it: Jirka Pelikán was dead. They found his lifeless body eventually, on the glacier at the foot of the face, and wept until the pain was gone. Then Josef ran to the other camps. "But there was no running away from it. And then the other expedition members' accusations followed, that somehow I was to blame for Jirka's death."

Later on, further accusations were to be leveled about the way in which the expedition had ended. Other members of the team continued with their own attempts on the route after a few days. Then a serac collapsed on the Sans Nom; although there were no serious consequences for the team, the motivation was now gone—suddenly the summit seemed impossibly far away.

Josef was the first to leave Base Camp; he had to inform the family about the tragic accident. "After 2 days I am sitting in a meadow, enjoying a fantastic view of Annapurna and Dhaulagiri. Both mountains are glittering in the sunlight and look so majestic, so peaceful."

Like Herzog before him in 1950, and many others after him, Nežerka was now confused and his emotions in tatters, happy and sad at the same time.

"The three of us have climbed a beautiful face and have had a fabulous time of it. Each of us was able to fulfill his desires. But we survivors have lost a good friend. I do not know to what extent I am to blame, but I will carry it with me forever."

Jindřich Martiš was also to lose his life in the Himalayas, in 1998, on a trekking trip to the Annapurna region.

Josef Nežerka concludes his successful, yet tragic, Annapurna story with the following words: "I do not know if it all makes any sense."

A RETROSPECTIVE

How often does Maurice Herzog, sitting in his chalet in Chamonix, think of the young men who set of for Nepal with him back in 1950—Couzy, Schatz, Terray, Lachenal, Rébuffat, Oudot, Ichac, and Noyelle? All of them have since died: Louis Lachenal in a crevasse in the Mont Blanc massif, Jean Couzy on a climb in the Vercours near Grenoble, Lionel Terray together with a young companion near Chamonix, Dr. Oudot in a car accident. The book *Annapurna,* a huge success, reminds us of them all.

Maurice Herzog's answer to the question whether he would dare to do it all again is, even today, a resounding "yes."

Despite all the pain?

Yes, in spite of the pain, even in spite of the vilification he was later to suffer, in spite of everything.

And his son? Would he ever encourage his children to head for the Himalayas?

He would not hold them back, but he would not encourage them. High-altitude mountaineering is dangerous. Moreover, Annapurna is still the most dangerous eight-thousander, as statistics have proved.

Are we then to attribute the 1950 success on Annapurna solely to the personal comittment of one Maurice Herzog and to his style of leadership? Did he really lead his expedition with the air of a Napoleon Bonaparte? "We must climb it, and climb it immediately." Yes; but we need to state here that toward the end of the expedition, Herzog was in a kind of delirium. The raw anger at searching in vain for so long for a possible route simply drove him too far.

Often the men set off walking in the morning and marched until darkness fell. They were under considerable time pressure, the clock was ticking. Each day, the clouds came in earlier as the monsoon approached. They climbed higher and higher, up the ice, through snowstorms and mist, up into that strange world beyond, a world that seemed not to belong to this planet of ours. Step by step, Herzog and Lachenal finally pushed on toward

The first postwar French expedition had two possible goals: Annapurna and Dhaulagiri. This was the first time that the hitherto forbidden frontier of Nepal had been breached. At the head of the expedition was a 30-year-old engineer. Maurice Herzog today.

the summit, Herzog climbing like a man possessed. And there Lachenal took that photograph of Maurice Herzog, the one that was to make him famous— the first man on the summit of an eight-thousander!

Lachenal and Herzog, the two " victorious summiteers," were living in different worlds up there, that much is certain. Lachenal wanted only one thing, to get back down to their top camp; Herzog, on the other hand, wished to enjoy the moment of victory. Under the impression that this was the most important moment of his life and to be enjoyed to the full, he stayed up there too long.

"Did I stay too long on the summit of Annapurna? Perhaps, but for me it was the great moment, the fulfillment of an ideal I had dreamed about since I was a young boy." I believe him, and I think he was well aware that they were the first people to have climbed an eight-thousander. "Surely one is allowed to enjoy a few moments of triumph on the summit?"

Maurice Herzog's hands and feet began to freeze up there, but the terrifying thought that they might not make it back down came only later. On the walk out from the mountain, Maurice Herzog was just a shadow of his former self. The expedition leader was suffering badly, with open wounds and frostbite. Villages in which there had been an outbreak of cholera had to be circumvented, streams and roads were rendered impassable by the monsoon rains. Often Herzog wished for just one thing: to be left behind to die.

Yet Herzog not only stayed alive, his book was translated into twenty-five languages and was published in more than 100 different editions. Through the sale of the rights to the book, the Himalaya Committee in France was able to finance further expeditions to the Himalayas, at least the bigger ones.

Maurice Herzog became a government minister. Under General de Gaulle, he spent eight years in charge of youth matters and sport in France. Later he became mayor of Chamonix.

It is without doubt a splendid biography. Maurice Herzog had indeed reached the summit of achievement—a mountaineering success story!

And now, with hindsight, how does he himself judge his life?

"I believe my life has been finer than I could ever have dreamed possible," he says, and after a pause, he continues, "Annapurna gave me something that nobody else could possibly imagine."

Twenty years after the "conquest of the summit," the search began for the difficult routes on Annapurna. Here, Hans Kammerlander climbs the upper seracs on the Northwest Face of Annapurna I (1985).

Porters on the approach march to Annapurna, with Dhaulagiri in the background

To the left, the glaciated North Face; to the right, the rocky Northwest Face of Annapurna I. The route takes a line up the back of the huge corner system and then up and left along the ridge to the Main Summit.

A whole series of routes now grace the South Face, which is more than 2 miles wide.

View from the West Ridge of the upper section of the South Face of Annapurna. In 1970 Don Whillans and Dougal Haston climbed the obvious snow gully on the right to a ledge on the ridge, continuing from there in a direct line to the summit.

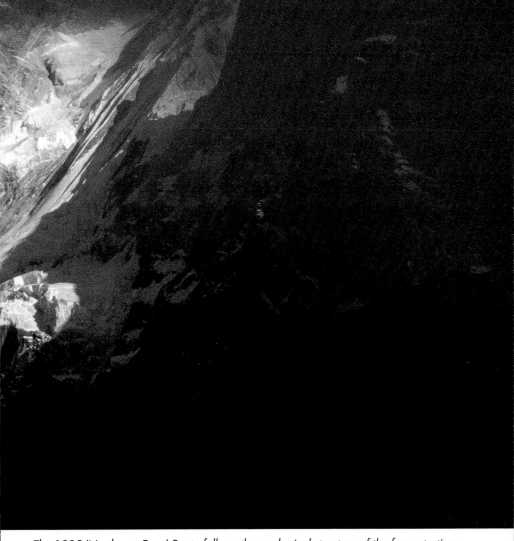

The 1985 (Northwest Face) Route follows the geological structure of the face, starting from the glacial basin (bottom left) and taking a rightward-trending ramp to reach the serac barrier at midheight. From here it climbs the sharp ridge up and left.

On his hands and knees, a porter crosses a wobbly bridge in the Miristi Khola.

The northern approach route to the foot of Annapurna I is still as arduous as it was in 1950, 1970, and 1985.

The porters take a rest break on the way to Base Camp. Behind them, in the haze of morning, is the Northwest Face.

A camp on the approach march, with the usual dusting of new snow that has fallen overnight

Base Camp beneath a canopy of prayer flags. In 1985 the camp at the foot of the Northwest Face was sited on dry ground between crags and the moraines.

Protected by a tower of ice, the first high camp sits beneath the Northwest Face of Annapurna.

Reinhard Patscheider goes to work on the ice between the foot of the face and Camp I.

Mixed ground on the Northwest Face at an altitude of almost 20,000 feet (6000 m)

Reinhard Schiestl in the icefall at the foot of the Northwest Face

For reasons of safety (rockfall) and because of the constant worry that a fall of new snow might make retreat impossible, fixed ropes were placed on the first third of the Northwest Face in 1985 to keep the line of descent back down to the valley open.

Reinhold Messner climbs the ice pitch between the corner and the first serac band.

The last section of the summit ridge (West Ridge), where it is usual to detour around onto the ledges on the north (left) side

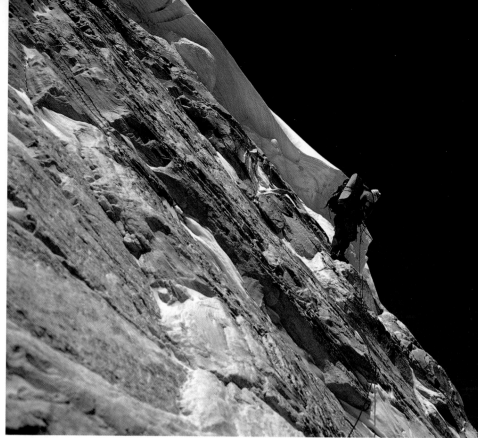

Hans Kammerlander in the middle of the sweep of slabs below the first serac band

View past the shoulder of the South Face toward Annapurna II, Peak 29, and Manaslu

Descent. Retreat from the steep face back to the foot of the wall, after days of living with high winds, new snow, and the ever-present danger of avalanches, was (and still is) like a kind of resurrection, like sunrise after a long, dark night.

FACTS AND DATES

Annapurna I, with the East, Middle, and Main
Summits; the West Shoulder (Sans Nom); and
The Fang, which was first climbed by Sepp
Mayerl with a team from East Tyrol—a masterful
achievement in classic mountaineering

ANNAPURNA CHRONICLE

Himalayan Mountaineering 2000: Mass Tourism

What changes have there been in the field of 26,000-foot (8000-m) mountaineering over the last fifteen years? The equipment has become even lighter and the collective knowledge about the Death Zone has grown, it is true, but the major change has been in the many different groups of people—commercial expeditions as well as national teams—now heading for the Himalayas, who lay seige to the highest mountains and leave a lasting impression on them.

Annapurna I from the south. Because this eight-thousander is much more easily accessible via the southern approach than from the north, the south side was well known before the north flank had even been seen. For a long time, however, the ascent of the mountain from the south was too difficult.

If, in the thirty years after Annapurna was first conquered, it was almost exclusively the elite of the classic mountaineering nations (England, France, Germany, Austria, Switzerland, Italy, the United States, and Japan) who were attempting the more difficult and higher challenges, climbers meanwhile have come from all over the world to climb here. Understandably, it was Mount Everest and the so-called "easy eight-thousanders" that were to attract the crowds; the result of all this attention was that the climbs ended up being preprepared both by and for these masses of people, becoming relatively easy to find and readily accessible, to the extent that even less talented climbers began to arrive on the scene, suddenly scenting an opportunity to set foot on the Roof of the World themselves. With super-lightweight oxygen apparatus, new types of medicines, preprepared trails, and camps at convenient intervals, it became an attractive proposition for more and more people to utilize the brief periods of fine weather to make a dash from the foot of the mountain to the summit and back. Nevertheless, tragedies did occur.

Soon the only ones accomplishing pioneering deeds in the Himalayas were the climbers from the former Eastern Bloc of Europe, who had much ground that they wished to make up after the collapse of communism and

The northern approach to Annapurna was familiar in 1950, to the locals at least, who used to herd their yaks up as far as the Thulo Begin in the summer. Herzog and his team followed the tracks of the shepherds and hunters right up to the Base Camp.

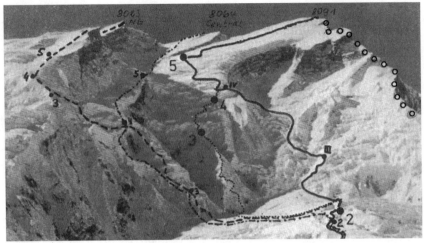

The North Flank, with the five different routes and camps marked:
————French Route 1950   — · — · — ·German Route 1980
— — — — —Spanish Route 1974   o o o o North Pillar 1996
·········· Dutch Route 1977

who were also the first to realize that it was not so much the height of the peak that counts as a sign of quality but the atmosphere of exposure that reigns up there.

This development in the area of 26,000-foot (8000-m) mountaineering has come about as a result of the fact that climbing has become a world-wide movement and also because people have kept quiet about the fact that the quality of the routes climbed will not necessarily be improved by an increase in the volume of traffic they get. It is just a shame that nowadays even those who profess to be making the "next steps" in high-altitude moun-taineering have to make their climbs amid the single-file lines of hordes who have reduced the eight-thousanders to prestige peaks for the masses.

Annapurna Climbing History

Although fifty years later, "the first eight-thousander," as Annapurna is of-ten called in climbing circles, has been climbed from every side, it has never become a fashionable mountain to climb. Annapurna remains a mountain to aspire to, but nowadays this has more to do with the difficult Big Wall climbing on the South Face than the height of its summit. No other eight-thousander has so many routes on it (including variations).

Height: 26,545 feet (8091 m)

Geographical situation: latitude 28 degrees 36 minutes north, longitude 83 degrees 49 minutes east; in the Nepalese Himalayas, between Kali-Gandaki and Marsiandi

It was only when he failed in his attempt on the Northwest Spur that Herzog turned his attention to the avalanche-prone North Face.

A view of the whole length of the South Face of Annapurna. This face will always be a magnet for the world's top mountaineers.

1950   Up to the spring of 1950, Annapurna was as good as unexplored from a mountaineering point of view. A French expedition, under the leadership of M. Herzog, having abandoned its original plan to climb Dhaulagiri, comes in from the west and reaches the glacial basin to the north of Annapurna, from where they finally spot a possible line of ascent up to a sickle-shaped glacier. Because the monsoon period is rapidly approaching, there is no time to lose. In spite of their haste, the too-short acclimatization period, and inferior footwear, M. Herzog and L. Lachenal dare to make an attempt on the mountain, and on June 3, 1950, they stand on the summit. Annapurna thus becomes the first eight-thousander to be climbed.

The descent, however, turns out to be anything but triumphal. With their control of the situation considerably impaired by a combination of drugs, altitude sickness, and an all-enveloping mist, Herzog and Lachenal return, together with their rescuers, visibly marked by their experiences of falling into crevasses, avalanches, and enforced bivouacs out in the open. The expedition doctor, Dr. Oudot, is even obliged to amputate frostbitten fingers and toes on the walk out.

1970   The second ascent of the Main Summit of Annapurna is achieved by a British Expedition, following the route climbed by the first ascensionists.

Shortly afterward, the famous partnership of D. Whillans and D. Haston makes the third ascent. The two men are members of a team

ANNAPURNA-I

In 1970 it was the year of the South Face. Could one have chosen a more beautiful, more featureless, and steeper wall for the start of the 26,000-foot (8000-m) Big Wall epoch?

Annapurna South Face, with the Bonington Route marked

of outstanding mountaineers with whom C. Bonington had set off for Annapurna, to make the first ascent of the exceptionally difficult South Face. They installed 14,765 feet (4500 m) of fixed rope on the 9,800-foot- (3000-m-) high, at times vertical, wall and it is this success that heralds the beginning of a new era in 26,000-foot (8000-m) mountaineering—the Big Wall era. This new style of Himalyan climbing gains widespread acceptance. I. Clough is tragically killed on the descent.

1974   A Spanish Expedition, led by J. Anglada, becomes the first to climb the 26,332-foot- (8026-m-) high East Summit of Annapurna.

1977   Dutch mountaineers establish a new route on the north side of Annapurna, avoiding the Sickle Glacier by detouring around to the left. Three men reach the summit.

1978   An American women's expedition also opts for the Dutch Route, with two participants and two Sherpas reaching the summit. One English woman and one American woman fall to their deaths.

1979   Two members of the sensationally hyped French Ski Expedition reach the summit via the original 1950 route. Y. Morin is killed on the descent.

Jordi Pons, the strongest man in Anglada's 1974 Spanish team

Annapurna I, seen from the northwest—the last of the faces to be climbed

Annapurna I, with the East, Middle, and Main Summits, viewed from the north

1981   A Polish expedition led by R. Szafirskis climbs the buttress on the right-hand side of the South Face. Two of the participants make the first ascent of the Middle Summit, 26,414 feet (8051 m), via a new route. A Japanese Expedition under the leadership of H. Yoshino places two pairs of climbers on the summit, via the British South Face Route.

1982   A British team finds a new and dangerous line on the South Face, to the right of the Bonington route. The expedition is aborted after

On the Annapurna Traverse, Loretan pitches the bivouac tent.

A. McIntyre is killed by rockfall. A few years later, two Spanish climbers complete this extremely difficult route in Alpine style.

1984   A group of Swiss climbers sets out to climb the often-tried East Ridge and the traverse to the Main Summit. E. Loretan and N. Joos reach the East Summit after only 3 days' climbing and continue over the Middle Summit to the Main Summit, from where they descend the Dutch Route, thus making a complete traverse of the three Annapurna summits, Alpine style.

1985   R. Messner, lead climber of a small team, makes the first ascent of the Northwest Face with South Tyrolean H. Kammerlander. They reach the summit on April 24.

1988   In the post-monsoon period, P. Schnabl leads a group of Czech climbers to the Northwest Face of Annapurna, one of a series of ambitious objectives (including Dhaulagiri and The Fang) of the expedition. Starting up the ice spur to the right of the Messner Route—first done by P. Gabbarrou and up which the French had reached the West

Mixed ground—rock and ice—on the middle section of the Northwest Face of Annapurna

Annapurna Northwest Face: the initial pitches up the snow slope

Shoulder, but not the summit, of the mountain—they then attempt to extend the route. After fixing ropes and placing two high camps on the first half of the face, J. Martiš, J. Nežerka, and the expedition doctor, J. Pelikán, push the route, with some very hard climbing up

Annapurna I and the West Shoulder (on the right):
○○○○○ *French Pillar (Sigayret) to the West Shoulder (1984)*
●●●●● *Kammerlander/Messner Route (1985), with the variation attempted by the second team (unsuccessful)*
━ ━ ━ *Gabbarrou Spur. Nežerka and Martiš used the spur to gain the West Shoulder, continuing along the West Ridge (Messner Route) to the summit (1988)*
━ • ━ • *North Pillar (1996)*

icefalls and rock steps, finally establishing a third camp at 23,294 feet (7100 m) on September 29. On October 1, Nežerka, Martiš, and Pelikán set off to make their summit attempt, but the length anddifficulty of the climbing, at an altitude of 26,000 feet (8000 m), force them to bivouac. Pelikán had previously, during the afternoon of October 1, decided to descend alone and had fallen to his death. On the morning of October 2, Nežerka and Martiš, who are unaware of the accident, stand on the summit of Annapurna I. They then retrace their steps back down to Base Camp. The body of J. Pelikán is found on October 4 at the foot of the face at a height of 16,730 feet (5100 m).

1996   After forty-five years and numerous attempts, the Northwest Pillar of Annapurna I, the line first spotted by Herzog in 1950, is finally climbed. An international expedition of ten climbers (eight Poles, an American, and a Ukrainian) led by M. Kochanczyk thus accomplishes this logical and safe route from the north, finding the

climbing to be extremely difficult. They use 6,500 feet (2000 m) of fixed rope on the Pillar and establish five high camps. On October 20, A. Marciniak and V. Terzyul make it to the summit after fixing the vertical rock section at 24,278 feet (7400 m). This route might well become the "Normal Route" on Annapurna I, for although it is far harder, it is also safer than the original route climbed by the first ascent party, because it has less rockfall and avalanches, and fewer crevasses.

*The Annapurna
summit massif from
the north*

Expeditions

By autumn 1999, there had been 120 documented expeditions to attempt various routes on the 8091-meter Annapurna I in north-central Nepal. The following data originates from Elizabeth Hawley's archives in Katmandu.

YEAR	SEASON	LEADER OF EXPEDITION	ROUTE	RESULTS
1950	spring	France	Northwest Pillar	failed attempt
			North Face	1st ascent
1961	spring	Germany	West Side	failed attempt
1965	spring	Germany	East Ridge	failed attempt
1969	spring	Germany	East Ridge	failed attempt
1970	spring	Great Britain	North Face	2nd ascent
1970	spring	Great Britain	South Face	3rd ascent; 1 death
1970	autumn	Spain	North Face	failed attempt
1973	spring	Japan	Northeast Pillar	failed attempt; 5 deaths
1973	autumn	Italy	Northwest Pillar	failed attempt; 2 deaths
1974	spring	Spain	North Face to Northeast Ridge	East Summit reached
1975	spring	Austria	Southeast Ridge	failed attempt; 1 death
1977	autumn	Holland	North Face, including rib east of French Route	4th ascent
1978	spring	Austria	North Face	failed attempt
1978	autumn	United States	North Face (Dutch Route)	5th ascent; 2 deaths
1979	spring	France	North Face	6th ascent (with skis)
1979	spring	Japan	North Face (Dutch Route)	7th ascent
1979	autumn	United States	North Face (Dutch Route)	failed attempt; 3 deaths
1980	spring	Germany	North Face (Dutch Route)	8th–9th ascents
1980	autumn	Germany	North Face (Dutch Route) North Face, east of Dutch Route	failed attempt Middle Summit reached; 1 death
1980	winter	Japan	North Face	failed attempt
1981	spring	Sweden	East Ridge	failed attempt

YEAR	SEASON	LEADER OF EXPEDITION	ROUTE	RESULTS
1981	spring	Poland	South Face	Middle Summit reached
1981	autumn	France	Northwest Pillar	failed attempt; 4 deaths
1981	autumn	Japan	South Face	10th ascent; 1 death
1982	spring	Austria/ Germany/ Switzerland	North Face	11th ascent; 2 deaths
1982	autumn	Great Britain/ Poland	South Face	failed attempt; 1 death
1982	autumn	Japan	North Face	failed attempt; 2 deaths
1983	autumn	Italy	Northwest Pillar	failed attempt
1983	autumn	South Korea	North Face (Dutch Route)	failed attempt; 3 deaths
1983	autumn	Yugoslavia	South Face	failed attempt
1983	winter	Japan	North Face	failed attempt
1984	spring	France/Canada	West-Northwest Spur	failed attempt; 2 deaths
1984	spring	Spain	South Face	Middle Summit reached
1984	autumn	Switzerland	up East Ridge, down North Face	failed attempt
1984	autumn	Japan/ Czechoslovakia/ France	North Face	failed attempt
1984	autumn	Switzerland	up East Ridge, down North Face	12th ascent; East and Middle Summits also climbed
1984	winter	South Korea	North Face (Dutch Route)	13th ascent claimed; Middle Summit allegedly climbed
1984	winter	France	North Face (French Route)	failed attempt
1984	winter	Japan	South Face	failed attempt
1985	spring	Italy/Austria	Northwest Face	13th ascent
1985	autumn	Switzerland	North Face	failed attempt
1985	autumn	Japan	North Face (Dutch Route)	failed attempt
1985	winter	Bulgaria	South Face	failed attempt
1986	spring	Bulgaria	South Face	failed attempt
1986	spring	Italy	North Face (French Route)	failed attempt
1986	autumn	Italy	North Face (French Route)	14th ascent
1986	autumn	France	Northwest Pillar	failed attempt; 1 death

YEAR	SEASON	LEADER OF EXPEDITION	ROUTE	RESULTS
1986	autumn	France	Northwest Face	failed attempt
1986	autumn	France	East Ridge	failed attempt
1986	autumn	Poland	South Face	permission obtained but no summit attempt made
1986	winter	Switzerland	South Face	failed attempt
1987	winter	Poland	North Face	15th ascent
1987	winter	United States/ New Zealand/ Great Britain	North Face	failed attempt
1987	spring	Spain	North Face	failed attempt
1987	autumn	Spain	North Face	16th ascent
1987	autumn	Spain	North Face	17th ascent

Ice climbing on the Northwest Face of Annapurna (1985)

YEAR	SEASON	LEADER OF EXPEDITION	ROUTE	RESULTS
1987	winter	Canada/ United States	East Pillar to South Face	failed attempt
1987	winter	Japan	South Face	18th ascent; 2 deaths
1987	winter	Japan	North Face	failed attempt
1988	spring	Mexico		permission obtained, but did not reach the mountain
1988	spring	France/Italy/ United States/ Czechoslovakia	South Face	19th ascent

– – – Czech Route, with the three camps and the bivouac site marked

●●●●● Patscheider, Schiestl, and Prem Darshano's attempted route (1985)

– • – • Kammerlander/ Messner link

YEAR	SEASON	LEADER OF EXPEDITION	ROUTE	RESULTS
1988	autumn	Japan	Northwest Pillar	failed attempt; 2 deaths
1988	autumn	Czechoslovakia/ Italy	Northwest Face	20th ascent; 1 death
1988	autumn	Spain	North Face	21st ascent
1988	autumn	Poland/ Great Britain/ Ecuador/ United States/ Italy	South Face to East Ridge	East Summit reached; 1 death
1988	winter	Bulgaria	South Face	failed attempt
1989	spring	Italy	Northwest Face	failed attempt
1989	spring	Austria	North Face	failed attempt
1989	autumn	Bulgaria	North Face	22nd ascent; 2 deaths
1989	winter	Bulgaria	South Face	failed attempt
1989	winter	South Korea	North Face	failed attempt
1990	spring	Great Britain/ New Zealand/ United States	North Face	failed attempt
1990	autumn	Spain	North Face	failed attempt
1990	autumn	South Korea	South Face	failed attempt
1990	autumn	Italy	North Face	23rd ascent claimed
1990	winter	Yugoslavia	West Face	no attempt made
			North Face	failed attempt
1990	winter	United States	South Face	failed attempt
1991	spring	Austria/ Germany	North Face	failed attempt
1991	spring	Germany	North Face	failed attempt
1991	autumn	South Korea	North Face	failed attempt; 6 deaths
1991	autumn	United States	North Face	failed attempt
1991	autumn	Spain	North Face	failed attempt
1991	autumn	Japan	North Face	failed attempt
1991	autumn	Austria	Northwest Pillar	failed attempt
1991	autumn	Poland/ Belgium/ Italy/ Czechoslovakia (Jarozsz)	South Face	23rd ascent; 1 death
1991	autumn	Poland/ Belgium/ Great Britain/ Germany/ Portugal (Wielicki)	South Face	24th–26th ascents
1991	autumn	USSR (Gloushkovski)	North Face	27th ascent

Memorial to the dead at Annapurna Base Camp

YEAR	SEASON	LEADER OF EXPEDITION	ROUTE	RESULTS
1991	autumn	USSR (Senatorov)	South Face	28th ascent
1991	autumn	Yugoslavia	West Face	failed attempt
1992	autumn	Slovenia/Croatia	South Face	failed attempt
1992	autumn	France	South Face	failed attempt; 1 death
1993	spring	China (Tibet)	North Face	29th ascent
1993	autumn	Slovenia	South Face	failed attempt
1993	autumn	Spain (Sune)	North Face	failed attempt
1993	autumn	Spain (Massegue)	North Face (Dutch Route)	failed attempt
1994	summer	Japan	North Face (Rib)	failed attempt
1994	autumn	South Korea	South Face	30th ascent
1994	autumn	France	South Face	failed attempt
1994	winter	South Korea	North Face	failed attempt; 1 death

YEAR	SEASON	LEADER OF EXPEDITION	ROUTE	RESULTS
1995	spring	Slovenia/ Croatia/ Mexico	North Face	31st–32nd ascents; 1 continuous ski descent
1995	autumn	France (solo)	South Face	failed attempt
1996	spring	South Korea	North Face	33rd ascent
1996	spring	Switzerland (almost solo)	North Face	34th ascent
1996	spring	Russia (Bashkir)	South Face	failed attempt
1996	autumn	Ukraine/Russia	South Face	35th ascent
1996	autumn	Poland/ Ukraine/ United States	Northwest Pillar	36th ascent
1996	autumn	Belgium	North Face	failed attempt
			Northwest Pillar	failed attempt
1996	autumn	France/Spain	South Face	failed attempt
1996	winter	South Korea	Northeast Pillar	failed attempt
			North Face	failed attempt
1997	spring	South Korea	Northeast Pillar	failed attempt; 1 death
1997	autumn	Italy	North Face	failed attempt
1997	autumn	Spain	North Face	failed attempt
1997	winter	Italy (Kazakh)	Southwest Pillar via East Face of The Fang	failed attempt; 2 deaths
1997	winter	Japan	North Face	failed attempt
1998	spring	South Korea	North Face	37th ascent
1998	spring	Italy/France	South Face	failed attempt; 1 death
1998	spring	Spain	North Face	failed attempt
1998	autumn	United States	South Face	failed attempt
1999	spring	South Korea/ Spain	North Face	38th ascent; 2 deaths
1999	spring	Spain	North Face	failed attempt
1999	autumn	???	???	permits obtained but no attempts made

Summit Successes

By autumn 1999, 101 men and 5 women had reached the Main Summit of Annapurna I. The following data originates from Elizabeth Hawley's archives in Katmandu.

CLIMBER	COUNTRY OF ORIGIN	DATE	ROUTE OF ASCENT
1. Maurice Herzog	France	June 3, 1950	North Face
2. Louis Lachenal	France	June 3, 1950	North Face
3. Gerry Owens	Great Britain	May 20, 1970	North Face
5. Don Whillans	Great Britain	May 27, 1970	South Face
6. Dougal Haston	Great Britain	May 27, 1970	South Face
7. Mathieu von Rijswick	Holland	October 13, 1977	North Face
8. Sonam Wolang Sherpa	Nepal	October 13, 1977	North Face
9. Irene Miller	United States	October 15, 1978	North Face
10. Vera Komarkova	Czechoslovakia	October 15, 1978	North Face
11. Mingma Tshering Sherpa	Nepal	October 15, 1978	North Face
12. Chewang Rinzing Sherpa	Nepal	October 15, 1978	North Face
13. Yves Morin	France	April 30, 1979	North Face
14. Henri Sigayret	France	April 30, 1979	North Face
15. Sezio Tanaka	Japan	May 8, 1979	North Face
16. Pema Sherpa	Nepal	May 8, 1979	North Face
17. Gustav Harder	Germany	May 1, 1980	North Face
18. Konrad Staltmayr	Germany	May 1, 1980	North Face
19. Ang Dorje Sherpa	Nepal	May 3, 1980	North Face
20. Karl Schrag	Germany	May 3, 1980	North Face
21. Wolfgang Broeg	Germany	May 3, 1980	North Face
22. Maila Pempa Sherpa	Nepal	May 3, 1980	North Face
23. Ang Tsangi Sherpa	Nepal	May 3, 1980	North Face
24. Hiroshi Aota	Japan	October 19, 1981	South Face
25. Yukihiro Yanagisawa	Japan	October 19, 1981	South Face
26. Wastl Woergoetter	Austria	May 4, 1982	North Face
27. Werner Buerkli	Switzerland	May 4, 1982	North Face
28. Thomas Haegler	Switzerland	May 4, 1982	North Face
29. Dawa Tenzing Sherpa	Nepal	May 4, 1982	North Face
30. Erhard Loretan	Switzerland	October 24, 1984	up East Ridge, down North Face
31. Norbert Joos	Switzerland	October 24, 1984	up East Ridge, down North Face
32. Reinhold Messner	Italy	April 24, 1985	Northwest Face
33. Hans Kammerlander	Italy	April 24, 1985	Northwest Face

CLIMBER	COUNTRY OF ORIGIN	DATE	ROUTE OF ASCENT
34. Sergio Martini	Italy	September 21, 1986	North Face
35. Fausto De Stefani	Italy	September 21, 1986	North Face
36. Almo Giambisi	Italy	September 21, 1986	North Face
37. Jerzy Kukuczka	Poland	February 3, 1987	North Face
38. Artur Hajzer	Poland	February 3, 1987	North Face
39. Josep Maria Maixe	Spain	October 8, 1987	North Face
40. Rafael Lopez	Spain	October 8, 1987	North Face
41. Juan Carlos Gomez	Spain	October 11, 1987	North Face
42. Francisco Jose Perez	Spain	October 11, 1987	North Face
43. Kaji Sherpa	Nepal	October 11, 1987	North Face
44. Noboru Ymada	Japan	December 20, 1987	South Face
45. Yashuhira Saito	Japan	December 20, 1987	South Face
46. Teru Saegusa	Japan	December 20, 1987	South Face
47. Toshiyuki Kobayashi	Japan	December 20, 1987	South Face
48. Benoît Chamoux	France	May 10, 1988	South Face
49. Nicolas Campredon	France	May 10, 1988	South Face
50. Steve Boyer	United States	May 10, 1988	South Face
51. Soro Dorotei	Italy	May 10, 1988	South Face
52. Josef Rakoncaj	Czechoslovakia	May 10, 1988	South Face
53. Jindřich Martiš	Czechoslovakia	October 2, 1988	Northwest Face
54. Josef Nežerka	Czechoslovakia	October 2, 1988	Northwest Face
55. Pablo Aldai	Spain	October 3, 1988	North Face
56. Juan Fernando Azcona	Spain	October 3, 1988	North Face
57. Ludmil Ianakiev	Bulgaria	October 28, 1989	North Face
58. Petar Panayotov	Bulgaria	October 28, 1989	North Face
59. Ognian Stoykov	Bulgaria	October 28, 1989	North Face
Giancarlo Gazzola	Italy	October 5, 1990	alleged North Face
60. Gabriel Denamur	Belgium	October 20–21, 1991	up South Face, down North Face
61. Bogdan Stefko	Poland	October 21, 1991	South Face
62. Krzysztof Wielicki	Poland	October 21, 1991	South Face
63. Ryszard Pawlowski	Poland	October 22, 1991	South Face
64. Rüdiger Schleypen	Germany	October 22, 1991	South Face
65. Wanda Rutkiewicz	Poland	October 22, 1991	South Face
66. Mariusz Sprutta	Poland	October 23, 1991	South Face
67. Gonzalo Velez	Portugal	October 23, 1991	South Face
68. Ingrid Baeyens	Belgium	October 23, 1991	South Face
69. Segey Arsentiev	USSR	October 24, 1991	North Face
70. Nikolai Cherny	USSR	October 24, 1991	North Face
72. Vladimir Obichod	USSR	October 26, 1991	South Face
71. Vladimir Baschkirov	USSR	October 26, 1991	South Face

Wanda Rutkiewicz, the most successful female high-altitude mountaineer to date, died on Kangchenjunga shortly after her ascent of Annapurna.

CLIMBER	COUNTRY OF ORIGIN	DATE	ROUTE OF ASCENT
73. Nikolai Petrov	USSR	October 26, 1991	South Face
74. Serguei Isaev	USSR	October 26, 1991	South Face
75. Akebu	China	April 26, 1993	North Face
76. Pemba Tashi	China	April 26, 1993	North Face
77. Ren Na	China	April 26, 1993	North Face
78. Tshering Dorjee	China (Tibet)	April 26, 1993	North Face
79. Park Jung-Hun	South Korea	October 10, 1994	South Face
80. Dawa Sherpa	Nepal	October 10, 1994	South Face
81. Ang Dawa Tamang	Nepal	October 10, 1994	South Face
82. Mingma Tamang	Nepal	October 10, 1994	South Face
83. Carlos Carsólio	Mexico	April 29, 1995	North Face
84. Davorin Karnicar	Slovenia	April 29, 1995	North Face
85. Andre (Drejc) Karnicar	Slovenia	April 29, 1995	North Face
86. Tomaz Humar	Slovenia	May 6, 1995	North Face
87. Park Young-Seok	South Korea	May 3, 1996	North Face
88. Kim Hun-Sang	South Korea	May 3, 1996	North Face
89. Kaji Sherpa	Nepal	May 3, 1996	North Face
90. Gyalzen Sherpa	Nepal	May 3, 1996	North Face
91. André Georges	France	May 15, 1996	North Face
92. Andrzej Marciniak	Poland	October 20, 1996	Northwest Pillar

CLIMBER	COUNTRY OF ORIGIN	DATE	ROUTE OF ASCENT
93. Vladyslav Terzyul	Ukraine	October 20, 1996	Northwest Pillar
94. Sergei Bershov	Ukraine	October 20, 1996	South Face
95. Igor Svergun	Ukraine	October 20, 1996	South Face
96. Sergei Kovalev	Ukraine	October 20, 1996	South Face
97. Han Wang-Dong	South Korea	May 3, 1998	North Face
98. Ang Dawa Tamang	Nepal	May 3, 1998	North Face
98. Phurba Tamang (second ascent)	Nepal	May 3, 1998	North Face
99. Arjun Tamang	Nepal	May 3, 1998	North Face
100. Kami Dorje Sherpa	Nepal	May 3, 1998	North Face
101. Juanito Oiarzabal	Spain	April 29, 1999	North Face
102. Fenan Latorre	Spain	April 29, 1999	North Face
103. Juan Vallejo	Spain	April 29, 1999	North Face
104. Um Hong-Gil	South Korea	April 29, 1999	North Face
105. Park Chang-Soo	South Korea	April 29, 1999	North Face
106. Ji Hyun-Ok (female)	South Korea	April 29, 1999	North Face
Ang Dawa Tamang (third ascent)	Nepal	April 29, 1999	North Face
Kami Dorje Sherpa (second ascent)	Nepal	April 29, 1999	North Face

Monsieur Annapurna

Maurice Herzog, born in 1919 in Lyon, France, has been actively involved in mountaineering since his youth. Together with Louis Lachenal he made several early repeats of classic routes on the Northeast Face of the Piz Badile and in the Mont Blanc region. After the war, when Jacques Cousteau set sail to explore the oceans and others were laying siege to the North and South Poles, Herzog had his sights set on the 26,000-foot (8000-m) peaks, none of which had then been climbed.

Herzog made a name for himself with the first ascent of this 26,000-foot (8000-m) mountain, and the near-tragedy that ensued, carving out a career in politics and high society. He was, and remains, a famous man in France—industrialist, Minister for Youth and Sport in de Gaulle's cabinet, Mayor of Chamonix, and "grand old man of mountaineering," known as "Monsieur Annapurna." His book *Annapurna* has become a worldwide best-seller and has sold more than a million copies.

The luck of being at the right place at the right time, and his motto of always putting everything he has into a project, have brought him a rich and full life. At the age of eighty, he is still a fit man and still full of enthusiasm—congratulations, M. Annapurna!

(Left to right) Reinhold Messner, Edmund Hillary, Maurice Herzog, and Chris Bonington attend an environmentalist conference in Japan. Maurice Herzog has dedicated his life to the mountains and mountaineering.

THE MOUNTAINEERS, founded in 1906, is a nonprofit outdoor activity and conservation club, whose mission is "to explore, study, preserve, and enjoy the natural beauty of the outdoors ...." Based in Seattle, Washington, the club is now the third-largest such organization in the United States, with 15,000 members and five branches throughout Washington State.

The Mountaineers sponsors both classes and year-round outdoor activities in the Pacific Northwest, which include hiking, mountain climbing, ski-touring, snowshoeing, bicycling, camping, kayaking and canoeing, nature study, sailing, and adventure travel. The club's conservation division supports environmental causes through educational activities, sponsoring legislation, and presenting informational programs. All club activities are led by skilled, experienced volunteers, who are dedicated to promoting safe and responsible enjoyment and preservation of the outdoors.

If you would like to participate in these organized outdoor activities or the club's programs, consider a membership in The Mountaineers. For information and an application, write or call The Mountaineers, Club Headquarters, 300 Third Avenue West, Seattle, WA 98119; 206-284-6310.

The Mountaineers Books, an active, nonprofit publishing program of the club, produces guidebooks, instructional texts, historical works, natural history guides, and works on environmental conservation. All books produced by The Mountaineers Books fulfill the club's mission.

Send or call for our catalog of more than 450 outdoor titles:

The Mountaineers Books
1001 SW Klickitat Way, Suite 201
Seattle, WA 98134
800-553-4453
mbooks@mountaineers.org
www.mountaineersbooks.org

Other titles you may enjoy from The Mountaineers Books:

HEROIC CLIMBS: A Celebration of World Mountaineering
Chris Bonington, editor
Encompasses the rich, broad spectrum of adventure that is mountain climbing in remarkable accounts by forty of the biggest names in modern mountaineering.

STORIES OFF THE WALL
John Roskelley
From his teenage climbing days to his twenty years in the Himalayas, Roskelley writes bluntly and honestly about his most significant influences on and off the mountain. A story of personal growth from one of the leading American mountaineers of his generation.

MOUNTAINEERING: The Freedom of the Hills, 6th Edition
The Mountaineers
The completely revised and expanded edition of the best-selling mountaineering book of all time; required reading for all climbers.

IN THE ZONE: Epic Survival Stories from the Mountaineering World
Peter Potterfield
True-life accounts of three climbers who faced the ultimate challenge in passionate pursuit of their sport: Colby Coombs on Alaska's Mount Foraker; Scott Fischer and Ed Viesturs on K2; and Peter Potterfield on Chimney Rock in the North Cascades.

SOUVENIRS FROM HIGH PLACES: A History of Mountaineering Photography
Joe Bensen
This unique book is a tribute to the parallel development of photography and mountaineering. Stunning photos and historical narrative make it a necessary addition to libraries of both photography and climbing fans.

EVEREST: The Mountaineering History, 3rd Edition
Walt Unsworth
The complete history of mountaineering on Mount Everest. This third edition is updated through 1999 and tells the unvarnished truth about many of the world's mountaineering heroes in their attempts to stand on the roof of the world.

REINHOLD MESSNER, FREE SPIRIT: A Climber's Life
Reinhold Messner
A chronicle of the remarkable career of one of the world's most innovative and disciplined climbers, the first man to summit Everest without supplemental oxygen.

THE BEST OF ROCK & ICE: An Anthology
Dougald MacDonald, editor
For more than twenty years, *Rock & Ice* magazine has published excellent writing from the world's best climbers. Now, for the first time, *Rock & Ice* editor Dougald MacDonald has gathered together a collection of the magazine's best essays.

GHOSTS OF EVEREST: The Search for Mallory & Irvine
Jochen Hemmleb, Larry A. Johnson, Eric R. Simonson
Members of the team who found Mallory's body on May 1, 1999, give the exclusive story of what they discovered on Everest and answer questions to the most enduring mystery in exploration history: Did Mallory and Irvine make it to the top? And, if they did, what happened to them?